Policy Creation and Evaluation

POCKET GUIDES TO
SOCIAL WORK RESEARCH METHODS

Series Editor
Tony Tripodi, DSW
Professor Emeritus, Ohio State University

RICHARD HOEFER

Policy Creation and Evaluation

Understanding Welfare Reform
in the United States

OXFORD
UNIVERSITY PRESS

OXFORD
UNIVERSITY PRESS

Oxford University Press, Inc., publishes works that further
Oxford University's objective of excellence
in research, scholarship, and education.

Oxford   New York
Auckland   Cape Town   Dar es Salaam   Hong Kong   Karachi
Kuala Lumpur   Madrid   Melbourne   Mexico City   Nairobi
New Delhi   Shanghai   Taipei   Toronto

With offices in
Argentina   Austria   Brazil   Chile   Czech Republic   France   Greece
Guatemala   Hungary   Italy   Japan   Poland   Portugal   Singapore
South Korea   Switzerland   Thailand   Turkey   Ukraine   Vietnam

Copyright © 2012 by Oxford University Press, Inc.

Published by Oxford University Press, Inc.
198 Madison Avenue, New York, New York 10016
www.oup.com

Oxford is a registered trademark of Oxford University Press

Library of Congress Cataloging-in-Publication Data

Hoefer, Richard.
Policy creation and evaluation: understanding welfare reform in the United States /
Richard Hoefer.
p. cm. — (Pocket guides to social work research methods)
Includes bibliographical references and index.
ISBN 978-0-19-973519-8 (pbk.: alk. paper)
1. Public welfare—United States. 2. Public welfare—Law and legislation—
United States.
3. United States—Social policy. I. Title.
HV95.H553 2012
362.5'5680973—dc22
2011012610
978-0-19973519-8

1 3 5 7 9 10 8 6 4 2

Printed in the United States of America
on acid-free paper

This book is dedicated to Paula Homer and Sharon Hoefer.
A portion of the royalties from the sale of this book will be donated
to Habitat for Humanity, an organization dedicated to improving
the lives of Americans who live in poverty.

Contents

Preface

When one person pays for another person's sustenance, often the former exerts a certain degree of control in their interaction. Parents believe they should tell their children how to behave, for example: when to come and go, what to believe, and whom to associate with. This principle of control following funding is even more applicable when organizations such as nonprofits and governments create policies that provide assistance, whether cash or in-kind. The great fear of those providing the help is that, rather than providing short-term aid to the unfortunate victims of bad luck or circumstance, that very funding promotes future reliance on more assistance. How to help out, without creating dependency, is the policy question that has never been satisfactorily answered.

Americans have struggled with this question since the first European settlers came to its shores. Early policy was along the lines of "Those who don't work, don't eat." In a wilderness, with starvation near at hand, each person was expected to contribute what he or she could in order to assure the survival of all. It was a communitarian result of individualistic efforts. As the number of people in English colonies grew, inevitably, the number of people who were not able to contribute much to the collective effort increased as well. Drawing upon their experiences in their homeland, a system of relief was instituted for the "worthy" poor—the elderly, widows, orphans, and persons with disabilities from birth, war, or accidents. The "unworthy" poor—those capable of work—received no handouts, lest such assistance become more attractive than earning a living for oneself and one's family by the sweat of the brow.

Centuries after these initial policies were implemented, policies remained similar. During economic downturns, whatever assistance that was provided to the unemployed and poor was still predicated on the distinction between those who were in their situation through no fault of their own, and those who should be doing something to lift themselves up by their own bootstraps. The cyclical nature of the capitalistic system that sometimes provided employment and sometimes did not was noted, but opportunities on the frontier was always there for the taking—one could make a life for oneself if only one put out sufficient effort.

During the 1930s, the United States once again confronted problems of unemployment and economic dislocation. This time, the response was different. The sheer magnitude of the Great Depression encouraged a policy response unlike that of past times. The threat of mass movements similar to the Communism and Fascism of Europe also provided an impetus to change course, if only to save capitalism from its own excesses. This new attitude was summed up in a presidential message by Franklin Delano Roosevelt several years after the Social Security Act of 1935 had been passed:

> Government has a final responsibility to the welfare of its citizens. If private cooperative effort fails to provide work for willing hands and relief for the unfortunate, those suffering hardship through no fault of their own have a right to call upon the government for aid. And a government worthy of the name must make a fitting response. (Franklin D. Roosevelt, *Annual Message to Congress,* January 3, 1938)

This approach, despite continued criticism from conservatives, continued to be the basis for at least some of the policy decisions of the American government for several decades. During the race for the presidency in 1960, candidate John F. Kennedy and his campaign manager and brother, Robert, were moved by the deep levels of poverty they encountered in places such as West Virginia, and among the elderly. Michael Harrington activated the nation's conscience with his 1962 book, *The Other America: Poverty in the United States.* Gradually, the economic support systems in the United States became broader, encompassing food assistance through the food stamps program, medical care through Medicare and Medicaid, and a certain level of income support through programs such as Aid to Families with Dependent Children and Supplemental Security Income.

Yet the underlying fear of creating dependency did not fade. During the presidencies of Ronald Reagan from 1980 to 1988, and of his former vice-president, George H. W. Bush, from 1988 to 1992, underlying antagonism to "welfare" became mainstream opinion. Conservative authors declared that welfare caused the poor to be poor and encouraged dependency, broken families, and out-of-wedlock childbearing. Liberal authors concluded that AFDC was a failed program that marginalized the poor, keeping them from participating fully in American life. Both sides wanted to change the system, but in radically different ways. Conservatives opted for eliminating the programs such as AFDC altogether, in order to provide the spur of increased poverty to goad the idle into economic effort on their own behalf and for their children. They did not consider the insistent barriers that keep people in poverty, such as poor education, lack of transportation, few opportunities for employment that matched their skills, and so on. Liberals focused on altering policies so that more social services were available, more employment supports were put into place, and effects of past discrimination were mitigated. They did not emphasize the increases in the percent of children born to single mothers, particularly into families that were already poor, the length of time that the long-term poor received government assistance, and other indicators that the individual program recipients might be part of the reasons for the welfare rolls' expansion.

Into this milieu of the early 1990s came William Jefferson Clinton, who vowed to "change welfare as we know it" in order to prevent continued reliance on government funds. Newt Gingrich campaigned for a Republican House of Representatives in 1994 with a "Contract with America" that included a proposal to change welfare policy in the United States. In 1996, President Clinton signed the fruits of his and the Republican Congress's Personal Responsibility and Welfare Reform Act, which did away with the concept that the poor in America were entitled to federal assistance. Attacked at the time as the worst decision he had ever made, and shameful, even now Clinton is castigated by certain commentators for "selling out the poor" (see, for example, coverage by MSNBC commentator Rachel Maddow, who said that "Bill Clinton was probably the best Republican president the country ever had if you look at the policies that he passed" [*The Rachel Maddow Show*, March 31, 2010]).

Because the purpose of this book is to illuminate academic ideas relating to policy creation and evaluation, I do not delve into the substance of the welfare reform debate at many points. Some readers may see it as a fault that I do not provide a clear commentary on what I see as the failings or successes of the policy. What I have learned from writing this book is that the truth about the motivations behind the policy's creation is hard to discern. Was this primarily a good-faith attempt to fix flaws in the system that did not encourage self-sufficiency? Or was it really part of a vast right-wing conspiracy to continue an assault on rights for women and people of color? I do not claim to know. The effects of welfare reform seem clearer to me—poor families, as a group, are by-and-large not less poor due to the policies embodied in the welfare reform legislation. Welfare reform changed welfare but it did not affect poverty. The economy, with its ups and downs, affects family income much more than does the Temporary Assistance to Needy Families program. Still, Aid to Families with Dependent Children was not a program that should be looked upon as helping poor families become well-off either. So, if the only two choices before me were to keep the old system, or move to the new, I would have a difficult time making that decision. Allowing poverty to continue is not good policy; allowing long-term aid receipt for those who can use education and training to work is not either. It is my hope that readers of this book will learn how to examine the policy creation and evaluation processes more skillfully and with the ability to help improve social policy so that the difficult problem of providing meaningful assistance to individuals and families who can benefit from such aid is solved. Using the techniques of evaluation to conduct research on some of the alternatives that have been and are being proposed and tried, and feeding those results back into the policy creation cycle, is a useful, if long-term, approach to improving the lives of many.

Between the time this book was conceived and the time it was completed, the most important health care legislation in the history of the United States was passed and signed into law. It would please me very much if this book is an inspiration for an analysis of that legislation and its effects at some point in the future.

A short discursion about the genesis of this book allows me to thank the people who provided the impetus and help I needed to make it a reality. In 2006, around the 10-year anniversary of welfare reform, I began to formulate an idea that the passage of the most important change in America's version of the welfare state in 60 years would be a good reason to explore the processes of social policy creation. I was reminded of a book I had read in my graduate school days, by Graham Allison, titled *Essence of Decision*, in which he described the Cuban missile crisis using three different frameworks. I thought it might be possible and instructive to explain the creation of welfare reform in a similar manner. In addition, given the large number of evaluations of welfare reform policies that had been performed, it also seemed important to link the two ends of the policy process—creation and evaluation. This idea percolated for years, shunted aside by other issues and concerns. In 2009, however, Tony Tripodi, the editor of this series of books, approached me to write a social policy book. When I pitched this idea, he was immediately encouraging. With support from Maura Roessner, editor at Oxford University Press, and several anonymous reviewers of the proposal, I began work. After the initial draft was submitted, a set of very helpful anonymous reviews came back to assist me in improving the manuscript. At this point, I enlisted my colleague Dr. Regina Aguirre to provide assistance in the revisions when it came to expanding the material on qualitative methods. Working from the base of material I had written, she had a hand in improving several chapters with her comments and made substantial improvements directly in Chapter 5, for which I am happy to share authorship credit. Whatever errors exist in the book, however, belong to me alone, not to her or others who provided their advice and wisdom.

In addition to the credit that belongs to my professional colleagues, the largest debt I owe is to my family, who had to put up with a distracted husband and hidden-away father. I hope the product of my efforts is worth the time spent on it away from them. Of course I also owe much to the members of my community, my country, and my world who suffer from poverty. In order to pay them back a portion of my debt, I am donating a portion of the proceeds from this book to Habitat for Humanity, an organization that helps low-income people build their lives by building, with them, affordable, quality homes. Such an approach is not *the* answer to ending poverty, but it is a good step in the right direction.

Rick Hoefer
November, 2010

Policy Creation and Evaluation

1

Social Policy Creation and Evaluation

Social policy is like the water fish swim in: ubiquitous, fluid, and behavior-shaping. For social workers, policy is everywhere, ever-shifting and affecting all their interactions with clients. Social policy texts acknowledge this situation and try to engage students in understanding what current policy is (though the policies themselves may have changed since the text was written). Many texts go beyond such a static understanding and provide information on how social workers can change policy as well. Few texts, however, attempt to do what this book intends, to provide an understanding of how to use decision-making models to understand the policy that is enacted and then how to evaluate the effects of those policies.

The format of the first part of the book is intended to be similar to the political science classic *Essence of Decision*, which has been described as among the most influential political science works written since World War II. In that book, Graham Allison and Phillip Zelikow (1999) explain the resolution of the Cuban missile crisis using three different models of decision-making: the rational actor model, the organizational process model, and the governmental bureaucracy model. Allison and Zelikow show how each model can be used to sift through the available evidence regarding what happened and why. The Cuban missile crisis almost led to nuclear war between the United States and the Soviet Union. It is no exaggeration to say that the fate of the world was in the balance. Allison and Zelikow provide their readers three different explanations of what happened during this pivotal two-week period in October of 1962. They show by example that there is not just one correct answer to the questions they pose. As with many things in life, complexity and differing viewpoints can prevent us from settling on a simple answer to a simple question.

The goal of the book you hold in your hands is similarly to describe and explain one of the most important policy decisions in the post–World War II era (albeit in domestic policy): the passage of the Personal Responsibility and Work Opportunity Reconciliation Act (PRWORA) of 1996, otherwise known as either the Welfare Reform law, or the Temporary Assistance to Needy Families (TANF) legislation. The decision-making models included to assist us in understanding the creation of TANF are the historical model, the politics and power model, and the rational actor model. All are used to address the question, "Why did the welfare reform law emerge the way it did?"

The models used in this book are not identical to the models Allison and Zelikow (1999) used, at least partially because foreign policy is not identical to domestic policy. In foreign policy, the stakes may be higher, the goals clearer (national survival is always the bottom line), and the key actors somewhat fewer than in domestic policy. In a pinch, Americans tend to rally around the president in times of peril, such as when President George W. Bush received a huge bump in approval ratings and support after the terrorist attacks on September 11, 2001. In February of 2001, shortly after his inauguration, 53 percent of Americans approved of the job President Bush was doing, despite the fact that he failed to receive a majority of the popular vote in the 2000 presidential race. A few weeks after the attacks, his ratings soared to 90 percent approval, the highest ever recorded (and bested his father's (President George H. W. Bush) rating of 88 percent approval immediately after the freeing of Kuwait from Iraqi occupation in 1991 (CBS News, January 16, 2009). The president is allowed to speak to the nation and all other countries as the preeminent leader. Few in positions of authority, even if of a different political party or philosophical orientation, directly contradict the president in a time of crisis.

Domestic policy, on the other hand, presents a wildly different story. Even when a crisis situation is invoked, presidents do not have carte blanche to decide which course to follow. Witness the many times when presidents Clinton, Bush, and Obama have tried to create a sense of urgency in domestic policy, only to find considerable opposition and lack of support, even from members of their own political party. President Bill Clinton tried to pass health care reform but was thwarted. President George W. Bush wanted to drastically alter Social Security but did not achieve any change. President Barack Obama's term of office is still young as this is written, and health care reform was passed, but given that he is trying to fix the largest economic downturn since the Great Depression of the 1930s and working on improving numerous other domestic policy arenas, all while fighting wars in Iraq and Afghanistan, it is safe to predict considerable resistance to legislation embodying his proposals at some point. Republican gains in the midterm elections of 2010 showed how uncertain progress can be in domestic policy. Not everyone believes the he or she is capable of international diplomacy, but nearly everyone has ideas for how to make this country's domestic policies better, particularly when it comes to welfare policy. So, it is necessary to approach domestic policy analysis and evaluation in ways at least somewhat different than foreign policy.

Various typologies of domestic policy have been created. One of the most commonly used was first described by Lowi (1964). He discusses three types of policy: distributive, regulatory, and redistributive. He indicates that the categories overlap to a considerable extent, in the long run, but also makes it clear that politics is much more about the short run than the long, so the distinctions are useful.

Distributive policy (also known as "pork barrel" policy) moves resources from one broad segment of society to a loosely tied set of individuals who receive the benefits. Costs are borne by many, while the rewards are garnered by a select few. As Lowi writes, "Distributive policies are characterized by the ease with which they can be disaggregated and dispensed unit by small unit, each unit more or less in isolation from other units and from any general rule. . . . They are policies in which the indulged and the deprived, the loser and the recipient, need never come into direct confrontation" (Lowi, 1964, p. 690). An example of distributive policy is agricultural subsidies, which are paid to individual farmers and corporations that own the land, coming from general tax revenues. Each of us who pays taxes contributes a small amount, while the benefits go to a relatively small group of dispersed and unconnected, yet easily identifiable, "winners." Other examples include tariffs (taxes paid on some imported goods that increase the costs of those products to the point that it is less expensive to buy similar goods made in the United States) and defense procurement programs that cause large amounts of military spending to occur in relatively few areas of the country. There are certainly clear winners and losers in these decisions, although, as Lowi mentions, while one might be a loser with one particular distributive policy, one can be a winner in another. The state of Kansas, for example, loses in regard to military procurement spending, but wins in regard to agriculture subsidy policy, compared to some other states. Senators and members of Congress have often been very diligent in ensuring that their state or district gets "its share" of federal spending.

Regulatory policy also has clear individual winners. The key difference between it and distributive policy, however, is that a regulatory policy decision is a clear choice between an individual (or class of individuals) who wins and an individual (or class of individuals) who loses, based on general rules or principles (Lowi, 1964). When clean air laws are applied, for example, the owners of cement-making plants may have to install expensive scrubbing equipment to ensure that the exhaust coming from a smokestack meets the new standards. This action causes the owners of cement factories to lose, but benefits everyone downwind of the plant. As a second example, when one of a strictly limited number of taxi licenses is given to one cabbie and not another (according to specified rules), a clear individual winner smiles and a clear individual loser grimaces.

Policy concerning social welfare programs such as we discuss in this book are labeled "redistributive" because resources are shifted from one clearly identified large group of people to another clearly identified large group of people. The groups are generally large enough to be considered social classes (Lowi, 1964). While actual redistributive effects of policies may be small, frequently the political battles around them are intense and partisan because of the fear of redistributive effects' being made stronger over time. These contending groups can be called the "haves and have-nots, . . . bourgeoisie and proletariat" (Lowi, 1964, p. 691). To its opponents, redistributive policy is seen as the tip of the spear of class warfare—it takes from the well-to-do and gives to the poor, weak, and ill. Examples of specific redistributive policies include the TANF program and even, to some extent, the Social Security retirement pension program that provides a relatively higher benefit for seniors who were low-wage earners compared to retirees who had higher incomes during their working years.

What makes this a very useful scheme to understand is that Lowi predicts that the politics of legislation is different depending on the type of policy debated. With welfare policy, as with all redistributive policy, "there will never be more than two sides and the sides are clear, stable, and consistent. Negotiation is possible, but only for the purpose of strengthening or softening the impact of redistribution" (Lowi, 1964, p. 712). As we look more deeply into the case of welfare reform in 1996, we shall see just how true these words are.

DEFINING AND DISCUSSING IMPORTANT TERMS

We will have much more to say about the models of domestic policy creation chosen for inclusion in this book later, but now we turn to defining and discussing important terms that will be used throughout.

Let us first define *social policy*. As in most things academic, the term has many definitions, and different authors defend their definition against all comers. Gilbert and Terrill (2009), when discussing the definition of terms such as *social policy* and *social welfare policy*, note that "no single definition is universally, nor even broadly, accepted" (p. 2). In order to assist in understanding what social policy is, before coming up with "the" definition of social policy to be adopted for this book, let us look at some of its more prominent characteristics.

- While social policy is generally considered to be the result of government action, it can also be created by nonprofit and for-profit entities (Alcock, 2008; Karger and Stoesz, 2010).
- Social policy can be created at local, regional, state, national, or international levels (Alcock, 2008; Blau, 2004).
- Social policy determines the major service goals of programs; the characteristics of who receives services; and the service options available for clients, among other things (Popple and Leighninger, 2008).

- The topics of social policy are related to fulfilling basic human needs, extending beyond what is termed social welfare policy, which concentrates on income maintenance, nutrition, physical and mental health, employment, housing, education, and the like (Blau, 2004; DiNitto, 2007).
- Social policy, as an academic subject, is interdisciplinary and uses tools and perspectives from many sources (Alcock, 2008).

While almost every author has an idea how to define the terms *social policy* and *social welfare policy*, for the purposes of this book, I prefer the following definitions for their simplicity and common-sense level of understanding. The definition of social policy adopted here is simply "the laws, regulations, and statements of authoritative organizations to promote well-being." Social welfare policy, a more restricted domain than social policy, is defined (following Dear's [1995] lead) as "those policies that affect the distribution of resources" (p. 2227).

Having now defined social policy (and also social welfare policy), we turn to the word *creation*. Clearly, this word comes from the verb *create*, which means "to cause to come into being" or "to evolve from one's own thought or imagination" (Dictionary.com, 2010). What is interesting, however, is that policy creation occurs as a group process, with many people having a hand in any policy's creation. In addition, there are often many antecedents for a "new" policy. One often finds that "new" ideas in social policy are retreads from other localities or times. This is not necessarily a bad thing, but it does take away some of the luster from the advocates who loudly proclaim that they have come up with something new.

Policy ideas that are touted as being new gain some of their cachet from analysis of new information, or the application of analytical techniques that have not been tried on old information before. *Analysis* is used to mean a systematic and rigorous approach to understanding a phenomenon. The key word here is *understanding*—after an analysis is completed (using systematic and rigorous techniques), we want to be able to say we know better how that phenomenon came to be, operates now, or may exist in the future.

Social policy creation, as understood in this book, is "a group process to develop laws, regulations, and statements for authoritative organizations to improve well-being, often using some type of analysis as a means of evidence and persuasion, and usually based on previous policies."

The processes by which social policies are created are inherently complex because they are group processes. As difficult as it may be to understand the thoughts, beliefs, attitudes, and behaviors of one person, the challenges become exponentially more difficult when examining group processes. In order to improve our ability to understand the social policy creation process, we must turn to theoretical models, which provide a way to simplify the immense complexities of the situation.

Theoretical models can be compared to different sorts of cameras. An ordinary digital camera looks at what is on the surface—a photograph will show what clothes a person is wearing, whether that person is smiling, or skin tone. An X-ray presents a different image, showing skeletal details (including whether bones are broken) and indicating something about internal tissue and organs. A CAT scan gives an entirely different sort of picture, enabling a skilled interpreter to understand the processes that take place inside the body. In essence, each image is accurate, but each is also quite different. Each is useful, but in very different ways.

Just as there are different types of images, there are different models to use when trying to understand policy creation. In order to be useful, a model should be systematic (meaning that there is a clear series of steps or questions to answer) and rigorous (meaning that high standards of evidence are required to accept something as true). In the next three chapters, for example, we will go through three analytical models to answer the question, "Why was welfare reform (officially the Personal Responsibility and Work Opportunities Reconciliation Act of 1996) created in the form that emerged?" Each model is described, along with a series of questions to answer. As each systematic model is used, different answers emerge. The point of this exercise is to show how the choice of model to understand a phenomenon affects the answers one receives. Model choice is not neutral—it has repercussions that a knowledgeable policy analyst should be aware of.

WHAT IS SOCIAL POLICY EVALUATION?

At the other end of the policy trail from creating policy is evaluation. Controversy exists as to whether program evaluation and social policy evaluation are the same, and whether either one (or both) are the same as research or policy analysis. Although the discussion of definitions of similar terms can be overdone (as we saw previously in defining "social policy"), especially when there is considerable overlap in the concepts, we will nonetheless take a brief look at the debate so as to lay out the parameters of this book.

Social policy research can be defined as the application of (qualitative and quantitative) research techniques to the topic of social policy. There is no particular demand on the researcher to provide a judgment regarding the value of the outcome of the research, although it is common for the write-up of the research to assess its limitations as well as the contributions it makes to the knowledge base on the subject. Program evaluation is also the application of research techniques. Still, as opposed to research, it is almost always expected to provide a judgment about the degree of implementation of the program that is being studied and the extent to which the program achieves the goals assigned to it. The differences between research and evaluation have been neatly summarized in this way: "Evaluation . . . requires the synthesis of facts and values in the determination of merit, worth, or value. Research, on the other hand, investigates factual knowledge but may not necessarily involve values and therefore need not involve evaluation" (Mathison, 2008, p. 189). This difference can be overstated, however, and not everyone agrees that there is much difference, particularly between evaluation and applied social policy analysis (Mathison).

Rossi, Lipsey, and Freeman (2004) describe program evaluation as more than using appropriate research techniques in looking at a policy or program. They define evaluation as "The use of social research methods to systematically investigate the effectiveness of social intervention programs in ways that are adapted to their political and organizational environments and are designed to inform social action in ways that improve social conditions" (p. 29). This places the activity of evaluation at the level of "the program," which is an "organized, planned and usually ongoing effort designed to ameliorate a social problem or improve social conditions" (p. 29). This would imply that the evaluation of policies (which may or may not be associated with a program) would be conceptually different, and perhaps require different methods, than *program* evaluation.

Later in their book, however, Rossi et al. (2004) further describe program evaluation as "a purposeful activity undertaken to affect the development of policy, to shape the design and implementation of social interventions, and to improve the management of social programs" (p. 370). Explicitly including policy in this way broadens the definition considerably, at least conceptually, although perhaps not so much practically speaking. Evaluation is thus an applied or practical activity, with its practitioners intending to have an impact on the world. Research, as an activity, does not necessarily have this as an intention (think of pure research in physics, for example), but in social work and other professions, research is often framed in practical terms like these as well.

According to a classic book in the field, one of the definitions of policy analysis is "the *process* through which we identify and evaluate alternative policies or programs that are intended to lessen or resolve social, economic or physical problems" (*emphasis in original*) (Patton and Sawicki, 1986, p. 17). This would not seem to be at all related to evaluation, except that the authors continue their discussion of policy analysis so that it includes analysis that is "done before or after the policy has been implemented" (Patton and Sawicki, p. 18). Furthermore, this after-the-fact analysis can be further broken down into two types: retrospective and evaluative, with "retrospective" analysis referring to the description and interpretation of past policies (What happened?), and "evaluative" policy analysis referring to program evaluation (Were the purposes of the policy met?) (Patton and Sawicki, 1986, pp. 18–19).

The bottom line of this short discussion is that the terms *evaluation* and *research* have large areas of overlap and, for our purposes, can reasonably be used interchangeably. In order to avoid constant repetition of the term *social policy evaluation*, this book will use the terms *policy evaluation*, *program evaluation*, and *retrospective* (or *evaluative*) *policy analysis* as synonyms, although many authors would disagree. The combined usage will mean the "rigorous and systematic collection of information to assess and improve at least one component of a social policy or program."

When we arrive at Part II of this book, we will examine the systematic and rigorous use of qualitative and quantitative data-collection methods that are the heart of policy evaluation, using examples from welfare reform research, and we will not make further distinctions between the many terms that are used in the field. This is because the purpose of all of these types of research, when looking at welfare reform and other policies, is to understand the facts of how policy change has affected clients' lives and the organizations that implement policies and to make judgments about these changes. For now, however, let us examine the placement of policy evaluation in the life cycle of social policy.

HOW SOCIAL POLICY CREATION AND EVALUATION INTERACT

Birkland (2005, p. 222) provides one commonly taught way to understand policy-making—the "stages model":

1. *An issue emerges.* This can occur through an emergency, a planned event, an effort by an issue entrepreneur, a regular report, or an action taken by government.
2. *The issue is put onto the decision-making agenda.* An individual or organization decides to make a decision about the issue.
3. *Alternatives are discussed, and one is selected.* A number of different ways to address the issue are brought forward.
4. *Enactment.* A process is used to make a decision to choose an alternative (which may be one of the original ideas, a new proposal, or a combination of elements of two or more alternatives).
5. *Implementation.* The chosen alternative is budgeted for, set into motion through hiring responsible staff and developing regulations, and, in general, action is taken to put the new law into effect.
6. *Evaluation.* The value of the policy is determined.

While the stages model is not a perfect approach to understanding policy making, it is useful in providing a heuristic level of analysis about where research on social policy can take place. A great deal of literature in political science and other disciplines has looked at what occurs in each of the listed stages. Policy creation, as defined in this book, can conceptually be linked to the first four stages listed by Birkland (2005), culminating in Stage 4, "Enactment," although policy creation continues into implementation, as that is where regulations and "street-level" policy are created (Lipsky, 1980). Policy evaluation is primarily at the last two stages Birkland listed, "Implementation" (because evaluation research can address issues of implementation as it occurs) and "Evaluation" of the effects of the policy, post-implementation.

Thus, creation is one point on a policy's life cycle. After several stages are lived through, an evaluation may be conducted to determine how well the policy was implemented, how effective it was in addressing its stated goals, and, sometimes, what unanticipated consequences also ensued. As this part of the cycle is completed, the information becomes part of the policy environment and may assist in keeping the policy alive as it is, making changes (either large-scale or small-scale), or perhaps killing the policy. It is thus of interest and importance to understand how evaluations can be and are actually conducted, because their design, write-up, and dissemination can have profound impact on policy decisions.

PLAN OF THE BOOK

This book has two parts. Part I uses different models of understanding policy creation to examine the question: Why did the 1996 Welfare Reform Law pass in the form that it did? After a short introduction to welfare policy in the United States from 1935 to 1995, each of the chapters uses a different approach to answer that question. Chapter 2 uses an historical perspective, Chapter 3 uses a politics-and-power perspective, and Chapter 4 uses a rational-actor approach. Each chapter provides a somewhat different answer to the question, despite having the same facts to work with. This shows the extreme importance of choosing one's analytical model carefully, because the questions one asks will determine to a high degree the answers one finds.

Part II turns to different questions: "Given that the 1996 Welfare Reform Law passed in the form that it did, how has it been evaluated and what have been its effects?" These questions are addressed (though not answered comprehensively) by seeking to understand the ways that qualitative (Chapter 5), quantitative (Chapter 6), and mixed (Chapter 7) research and evaluation methods can be and have been used.

Part I

Social Policy Creation

An understanding of the history of cash assistance in the United States is important to attain, before jumping into the rest of the book. This introduction to Part I discusses the history of the Aid to Dependent Children (ADC) program, which turned into the Aid to Families with Dependent Children (AFDC) program, which was then ended and replaced with the Temporary Assistance to Needy Families program. While one cannot always believe that the title of legislation is truly a reflection of its content, in this case one can read the names of the programs and see that the programs are reaching for different goals. The first program (ADC) is directed at supporting poor children; the second (AFDC) is aimed at the families who have children in need; and the third (TANF), while also aimed at families in need, is *not* going to be a permanent source of aid to those families.

While the TANF program is rightly considered revolutionary in terms of its ending 60 years of cash-assistance entitlement, we can learn from the program's precursors that some of the points of dispute in 1996 were points of dispute for the three-score years before that landmark legislation as well. Americans have often debated who was "worthy" of receiving government aid and who was "unworthy." The overall contours of the debate have not changed very much across the decades, but the details of the programs developed within those larger limits have caused considerable controversy. What follows is a quick overview of some of the most important aspects of the legislative history of federally subsidized cash assistance in the United States since 1935. One recurring theme to note is the swinging of the pendulum in terms of who should be eligible to receive benefits; another is the extent of work requirements; and a third is the circumstances under which people receiving benefits should be excused from working.

AID TO DEPENDENT CHILDREN

Aid to Dependent Children (ADC) was created as Title IV of the Social Security Act of 1935. It built upon the experience of states that had enacted "mothers' pensions" to assist children whose fathers were no longer in the home. Although a piece of federal legislation, it was designed to maintain the power of states to provide assistance to poor people within their borders rather than imposing a national standard for providing aid. Its main aspect was to allow states to use a mixture of federal and state funding to pay cash benefits to children whose parents were dead, incapacitated, unemployed, or absent from the home (Office of Human Services Policy, 2009).

States had a tremendous amount of discretion when it came to developing their ADC programs. While the federal government assisted in paying for the program (in the original legislation, up to one-third of state costs, with a maximum state payment of $18 for the first child in a family and $12 for each additional child), it had little influence over the way a state spent the funds, other than in determining the maximum amount of income a family could earn and remain eligible for the program.

States defined "need," set their own benefit levels, established (within federal limitations) income and resource limits, and administered the program or supervised its administration. States were entitled to unlimited federal funds for reimbursement of benefit payments, at "matching" rates that were inversely related to state per capita income. States were required to provide aid to all persons who were in classes eligible under federal law and whose income and resources were within state-set limits (Office of Human Services Policy, 2009, "Overview").

The law was seen as a stopgap measure to protect children whose fathers had died before becoming eligible for the full Social Security

Survivor's benefits provision. As more and more fathers worked long enough, it was foreseen that the need for ADC would gradually diminish and perhaps even become nearly unnecessary (DiNitto, 2007). At this time in the Great Depression, with state budgets under heavy strain from the millions of unemployed, states were very willing to accept federal dollars in this new program. By 1939, all (except eight) of the states had adopted an ADC plan for their state.

One of the key provisions of the 1935 law was that families with an unemployed father living in the home were not eligible for aid. The underlying premise was that, even in the Depression, with unemployment rates of nearly 25 percent (in 1933) (Bureau of Labor Statistics, 2003), the father should take any work to support his family. Any provision of cash in lieu of working could undercut the work ethic and promote dependency (a fear that remains potent in discussions of welfare and cash assistance programs).

According to the Office of Human Services Policy (1998), other provisions of the original legislation included the following:

- Funds were provided to assist children, not adults, although children were required to live with a parent or other close relative to be eligible.
- The federal government was empowered to create rules to administer the program.
- Each state was required to designate a single state agency to administer or supervise local administrative bodies in its state.
- If the state had the ADC program at all (and states were not required to have an ADC program), it had to be available in all parts of the state and the rules had to be applied consistently (that is, localities could neither add to nor ignore state provisions).
- States were required to set standards relating to eligibility standards, such as amount of property that recipients could own, and how to treat any earned and unearned income.
- Each state was allowed to set its own need standard (roughly speaking, how much it cost to live in that state at a minimal level) and payment level (the amount of funds that would be given to eligible people, which did not have to equal the need standard, and frequently did not).
- Children were eligible for aid through the age of 15.

Over the years, many of the law's specific provisions were altered, but the basic structure of the program was maintained. States received funding from the national government according to a specific formula to assist poverty-stricken people in their state, but the states themselves determined the exact eligibility standards and payment levels.

As time passed, some states became relatively more generous, while other states became relatively tightfisted. By 1996, the need standard varied greatly between states, and there was little correspondence between what was declared to be the lowest amount of monthly income to live in the state at a minimal level and the amount that was available in cash from the state. The state with the lowest acknowledged level of need for a family of three was Indiana ($320); the state with the highest was New Hampshire ($2,034) (Office of Human Services Policy, 1998, pp. 72ff). The corresponding average basic family benefit for these states shows a gap between what was needed (according to the state) and what was provided by the state: Indiana provided an average family benefit in 1996 of $239 (a gap of $81 per month) with a maximum benefit possible of $288. New Hampshire provided an average of only $434 (a gap of $1,600 per month) with a maximum benefit of $550. The state of Mississippi had the lowest average family payment ($118 per month) of the 50 states as well as the lowest maximum benefit ($120) (Office of Human Services Policy, 1998, p. 76). Of course, benefits from other programs (such as food stamps, Medicaid and Section 8 housing) decreased the gap between the need standard and the AFDC cash benefit, but even so, these program benefit totals did not usually equal the need standard. Disagreement over how to value the benefits (such as food stamps and Medicaid) made debates inevitable about whether benefits were "adequate."

Beyond dispute, however, was the fact that benefits to the poor did not keep pace with inflation. As the Office of Human Services Policy stated, when discussing the time period between 1972 and 1996, "For most of the time and in most of the states AFDC payment standards were declining when adjusted for inflation" (Office of Human Services Policy, 2009, p. 90).

Some of the changes to the original ADC program, and when they happened:

- In 1956, social services to ADC recipients were first authorized for federal reimbursement (at 50 percent); in 1962, the reimbursement rate increased to 75 percent, and the total amount of funds available to states was uncapped. This led to widespread abuses by state programs (Derthick, 1975), so, in 1975, the Social Services Block Grant was created to limit federal expenditures.

- Work requirements were first introduced in 1961 as part of the creation of the "unemployed parent" provision, whereby states were required to deny assistance to a family if an unemployed parent refused to accept work without "good cause."

AID TO FAMILIES WITH DEPENDENT CHILDREN (AFDC)

In 1962, the program's name was changed to Aid to Families with Dependent Children (AFDC) to signify the intention to provide assistance to parents, even unemployed parents, and that states could receive federal reimbursement for some of these costs (this was a state option to adopt, not a requirement, until 1984 when it became mandatory because states were dropping their participation in the AFDC-Unemployed Parent program due to high costs associated with the economic downturn of the early 1980s):

- The age of the child was increased to maintain eligibility up to age 18, or longer if the child was in school, until 1981, when the age limit became 18 years (or 19, if the child was still in high school and the state so decided).
- In 1962, Congress created the "Community Work and Training" program to provide jobs at prevailing wages to all post–18-year-old recipients of AFDC. At this point, refusing a training position meant losing one's eligibility for benefits.
- Work requirements increased over the years before the 1996 Personal Responsibility and Work Opportunity Reconciliation Act (welfare reform), including programs such as the Work Incentive Program (WIN), Program for Better Jobs and Income (PBJI), the Job Opportunities and Basic Skills Training (JOBS) program and the efforts under the Family Support Act of 1988 (Office of Human Services Policy, 1998).
- During the 1990s, portions of the federal requirements under AFDC were increasingly being waived in order to allow states to

> experiment with different levels and types of incentives and punishments to increase the amount of work, decrease dependency, and improve the morality of welfare recipients (Office of Human Services Policy, 1998).

These program alterations, in conjunction with economic and societal changes, caused caseload fluctuations over time (Office of Human Services Policy, 1998). In the 1960s, up to 1967, growth in the number of recipient families was slow and steady. From 1967 to 1973, growth was rapid. By 1977 there were nearly 3.6 million families on AFDC. For a number of years, case numbers fell and rose, although the recipiency rate (percent of the total American population in the program) remained between five and seven percent, depending on national economic conditions. Beginning in 1990, the number of families increased, reaching to over five million families in 1994, the highest year on record.

This growth was probably responsible for the increasing demands for change in the AFDC program by conservative researchers such as Lawrence Mead (1986) and Charles Murray (1984). Sensing political benefit, presidential candidate Bill Clinton promised to "end welfare as we know it" in his campaign of 1992, and Representative Newt Gingrich made welfare reform a key point of the 1994 congressional elections by including it in the Contract with America. Somewhat ironically, welfare rolls declined rapidly in 1995 and 1996, falling to levels not seen since 1991, at the time of the signing of the 1996 welfare reform law (otherwise known as the Personal Responsibility and Work Opportunity Reconciliation Act of 1996).

This information on welfare policy in the sixty years leading up to the creation of the PRWORA is provided to allow for better comprehension of the swirl of policy debate occurring during the summer of 1996. Given this context, we ask ourselves the same question three times, choosing a different model to enrich our understanding each time: "Why was the TANF bill passed the way it was, when it was?"

2

Using the Historical Approach

Social work and other policy disciplines have fine examples of historical analyses of social welfare policy (see, for example, Day, 2008; Hill, 2006; Jansson, 2008; Skocpol, 1995; and Trattner, 1998; among others). Histories of various societies and countries go back far into ancient times—we still have available to us the work of ancient historians such as Pliny and Plutarch, Herodotus and Thucydides, who were struggling over 2,000 years ago with the same need to capture and explain events that happened in prior years.

This chapter describes the historical approach to understanding social policy, what types of information are needed to use this approach, and the strengths and critiques of the approach as a means of understanding policy creation efforts and outcomes.

DESCRIPTION OF THE HISTORICAL APPROACH

At its heart, the historical approach to policy analysis is the telling of a story based on credible sources. It is often qualitative, almost journalistic, in nature. McNabb (2004) states: "Political history is the record of past or current political phenomena. It is composed of the recorded story of politics, political institutions, and the actors in the political world"

(p. 380). Historical policy analysis can use numbers and statistics as well (Feinstein and Thomas, 2002).

According to Howell and Prevenier (2001), the modern idea of scientific history writing was created by Leopold von Ranke (1795–1886). "In Ranke's view, history was a learned craft, the science of 'telling things as they actually occurred,' of insisting that 'if it is not in the documents, it did not exist'" (p. 12). Thus, the study of history became part of the positivist paradigm's approach to research, relying on the idea that one could understand the world through an objective analysis of verifiable and observable facts and artifacts (Howell and Prevenier).

McNabb (2004) identifies three methods used in historical research. The first is the *hermeneutic* approach (also called the "interpretive approach" [Denzin, 2002]), which examines in detail the leaders of countries and organizations to determine what they did and what they believed. "Hermeneutics is a way of interpreting historical documents and other phenomena in light of the events that took place at the time of the writing of the text, as well as approaching the interpretation from the intent and experiences of the text's author" (McNabb, 2004, p. 373). This often employs the qualitative approach to content analysis. As defined by Patton (2002), "content analysis is used to refer to any qualitative data reduction and sense-making effort that takes a volume of qualitative material and attempts to identify core consistencies and meanings" (p. 453).

It is important to place documents and other sources in their historical context so that we better understand a policy's intent. To understand the origins of American social security policies in the 1930s, for example, researchers must comprehend the extent of the Great Depression, the growing threat of fascist and communist political beliefs in the United States and abroad, and even the popularist heroes of the times, such as Huey Long and Father Charles Coughlin. Only by knowing about these matters can one fully comprehend the desire by Democrats and President Franklin D. Roosevelt to shape and then pass the Social Security Act of 1935 near the end of Roosevelt's first term in office.

Veit-Wilson (2000) provides an example of the hermeneutic approach to historical research that examines the problem of defining *welfare state*. He stresses the point that the term is loosely applied to any state where assistance is given, lacking a classification system where effectiveness and the amount of assistance are taken into account. Veit-Wilson examines misuse of the term, providing extensive examples, and then taking the reader on a historical journey of definitions of the term. Finally, he presents important aspects of the definition that need to be developed through research. This is an example of how social policy analysts using historical policy and qualitative content-analysis techniques can hope to clarify current policy debates by working toward a language that is concise and empirically grounded.

The second approach is *nomological*. This approach looks for generalities in history, seeking to uncover "laws" of history to explain what has occurred (McNabb, 2004). Using the quantitative techniques of economics and behavioralist social science, people using this approach to history "develop mathematical models to analyze dependent and independent variable relationships" (McNabb, 2004, p. 373).

Feinstein and Thomas (2002) provide an example of nomological historical research that examines the effects of policy. Their research examines whether the provision of outdoor relief to able-bodied workers during the early part of the 1800s in Southern England under the old Poor Law led to earlier marriage and more children (and thus higher costs to government) (Boyer, 1990, cited in Feinstein and Thomas, 2002). In the end, "The important conclusion from this study is that the provision of child allowances did have a positive effect on birth rates, other things being equal, and that the quantitative impact was large" (Feinstein and Thomas, 2002, p. 478). While it is not clear the extent to which Boyer believes Americans of the late twentieth century behaved similarly to the people of Southern England of the early nineteenth century, he, or someone else reading his work, might see many similarities. Such a conclusion would have bearing on the type and amount of child allowances or support for families that the U.S. government should provide. Just as Malthus suggested in the 1800s that providing more money for additional children would lead to large numbers of children living in poverty, conservative politicians of the 1990s declared that government funding of the Aid to Families with Dependent Children program was causing poor women to have additional babies. This is an example of how social policy analysts using historical policy and quantitative research techniques can hope to bring numerical arguments to bear on current policy debates.

Nomological policy studies that are quantitative in this way share the strengths and weaknesses of most quantitative research. Careful attention must be paid to the validity and reliability of measures, the representativeness of data (counter-evidence may have disappeared, for example), and the correct choice of design and analysis techniques.

The third approach discussed by McNabb (2004) is the *critical* approach to analysis—it "views all social phenomena and historical events from the point of view of continually changing systems of social relationships and dependencies" (McNabb, 2004, p. 373). Marxist and feminist scholars, despite their differences, both use a critical approach in their writing about social policy. Phyllis Day, for example, makes it very clear that her critical interpretation of history includes at its core

> those involved in the social welfare institution not as wielders but as sub-jects/victims/recipients/clients. It seeks to redress in part the loss of history for women, nonwhite people, and other groups oppressed by social institutions, and to relate intimately the place of the labor force and working people with the social welfare institution (Day, 2008, p. xv).

Blau and Abramovitz (2010) combine hermeneutic and interpretive analysis with a critical approach. They describe a model of social policy change resting on the economy, politics and the structure of government, ideology, social movements, and history and use this model in a qualitative way to critically examine several social policy areas. They show how social policy has been detrimental to the lives of several disenfranchised groups, such as Native Americans, African Americans, and women.

A general approach to historical research, as described in McNabb (2004), indicates that three steps should be followed: (1) gather data, (2) evaluate the information critically, and (3) present the facts and conclusions. This is a rather general description of the process, and it leaves considerable doubt about what constitutes good data, how to evaluate what is gathered, and how best to present the information. A more directive set of four steps for conducting historical analysis of social policy context is proposed by Spano (2000, p. 44).

1. Identify the relevant actors, their areas of contention, and how they define the problem.
2. Examine sources to try to understand why the issue is being considered at that particular time in history. Determine if it is a new problem and what specific events may have sparked the policy debate.

3. Discern the ideology behind the policy positions.
4. Try to identify similarities and differences in the political context between the social policy conflict under study and previous efforts to address the topic. What may have led to th resurgence of policy debate regarding this topic?

INFORMATION NEEDED TO USE THE HISTORICAL APPROACH

One of the key questions within historical research is, what is a reliable source of information? Sources are one of two types, according to Howell and Prevenier (2001): "remains" and "testimonies of witnesses." *Remains* are things that exist that are the result of processes such as building, hunting, cooking, and so on. *Testimonies* are "oral or written reports that describe an event, whether simple or complex" (p. 17). Usually, neither remains nor testimonies are created specifically to be historical sources— they are usually meant for some practical purpose at the time of their creation. The first issue for historical analysis is to find sources. In policy analysis, testimonies are by far the most often used source.

For people studying the more distant past, the key problem is usually finding sufficient source material. For people studying recent events, however, the key problem is usually discerning which of the myriad sources to use and which to ignore. An additional problem with analyzing more current policies is that new sources are constantly coming to light: examples include biographies or autobiographies of key actors; documents only recently declassified, released from quarantine, or cataloged in a presidential library; and misplaced material in private hands.

Four characteristics of sources' quality are important: "authenticity, credibility, representativeness, and meaning" (Burnham, Lutz, Grant, and Layton-Henry, 2008, p. 208). *Authenticity* is whether or not the document is what it purports to be. It is a type of validity measure: has the document been forged, altered, or amended in a surreptitious way? The authorship of the source bears on its authenticity and may also be in question. Did the purported author actually create the material? *Credibility* is related to but separate from authenticity. It refers more to whether the information in the source is believable. History is full of examples of people who authentically wrote memoirs, but whose words were met with skepticism. Even without meaning to deceive, people can sometimes inflate their own importance in shaping a policy decision. But that does not necessarily mean that other people agree with that assessment.

Representativeness is easy to understand but difficult to determine. In essence, the representativeness of a source is the degree to which it is congruent with the full range of sources. This is the reason to prefer using many sources of information to only one or a few (e.g., triangulation). One can only get an estimate of the degree of representativeness of a single source if one has sifted through the information from many sources. Sometimes sources disappear due to accidents, such as fire, or intentional destruction, such as shredding. Thus, the person looking at a source's representativeness must at least consider whether the source being examined, while representative of the material *still* in existence, may yet be unrepresentative of the information that *once* existed.

But the existence of a source that is authentic, credible, and representative is not enough. The analyst must determine its *meaning*, and thus there is interpretation involved. Indeed, in a hermeneutic vein, Howell and Prevenier (2001) write:

> Historians must always consider the conditions under which a source was produced—the intentions that motivated it—but they must not assume that such knowledge tells them all they need to know about its reliability. They must also consider the historical context in which it was produced—the events that preceded it, and those that followed, for the significance of any event recorded depends as much on what comes after as it does on what comes before (Howell and Prevenier, p. 19).

Thus, while it is up to the historical researcher to give the source its meaning, the historian is not free to invent things that did not happen or to assume things that are not there. Furthermore, historical researchers always *interpret* their sources. When historical researchers disagree, it is most often a debate about the meaning of remains and testimonies, not whether those remains and testimonies exist.

To show just how important interpretation in historical research is, let us compare two accounts of the running of the Children's Aid Society by Charles Loring Brace. One account says:

> Although many states established orphanages during the eighteenth century, current child welfare policy in the United States had its origins in

the 1870s. The large number of child paupers led Charles Loring Brace, founder of New York's Children's Aid Society, to move thousands of children from deleterious urban conditions in New York City to farm families in the Midwest. Eventually, criticism of Brace's methods, which were divisive of family and community, contributed to more preventive approaches to children's problems (Karger and Stoesz, 2010, p. 386).

Compare this to another account, which presumably has the same sources to rely on:

> Perhaps the best known child-saver was Charles Loring Brace, who began the Children's Aid Society in 1853 (a national private agency that merged with Family Services in the 1960s). Brace believed that pauper families should be prevented from getting any kind of relief that would keep them together. His solution was to relocate children with families in the West, where they might learn the benefits of hard work in an untouched environment. For twenty years, haphazardly and without follow-up, often simply "taking" (kidnapping) children they felt were in need, agents loaded children on trains and shipped them to cities in the West, where they were "picked over" and chosen by families. Unfortunately many families just wanted the extra help and badly mistreated the children. Many simply disappeared, either running away, getting lost, or dying. More than 50,000 children over a twenty-five year period were shipped to the West, from 4,000 a year in the 1870s to about 500 in 1892 (Day, 2008, pp. 234–235).

The two accounts agree on some details. Charles Loring Brace started the Children's Aid Society in New York City, and it was responsible for the transfer of thousands of children from there to families west of New York. Otherwise, the two accounts have little in common. Karger and Stoesz' depiction is about half as long as Day's and thus contains far fewer details. It is also more neutral to positive in tone, putting Brace's actions in a positive light (moving children from "deleterious conditions"). While stating that Brace "received criticism," the authors do not lend any support to such criticism. Day, on the other hand, discusses the situation in such a way as to lead the reader to be outraged by Brace's actions: his efforts were done "haphazardly and without follow-up," children were "kidnapped" and "shipped" to families in the West, some of whom "badly mistreated" them.

The stark divergences shown by this example exemplify the power of source interpretation. People involved in writing history must acknowledge the difference between the "objective sources" used and the interpretation of those sources, which has been created in the mind of the historian. Still, the historical approach to policy research does not allow just any interpretation to be set forth. There are standards by which interpretations are judged. If an interpretation goes beyond these standards, it is generally rejected (for example, people who claim the Holocaust did not occur in Nazi Germany are simply not taken seriously by historians). The standards used in historical policy analysis are intended to provide validity (truth) to the description of what occurred and also reliability (agreement between independent observers).

The primary technique in historical analysis is to find and then compare sources. Usually, someone writing a history of an event or series of events will prefer to consult with several sources rather than only one. This can create a problem, however, in that the sources may disagree about "what happened" or "why something happened." It is then up to the historian to deal with the discrepancies. The following paragraphs provide guidance to the historical policy analyst when comparing the information from multiple sources.

When all sources agree: In this situation, one can typically assume that whatever is being agreed to actually occurred (or did not occur); but this may not be true, if all the sources are really from one underlying and incorrect source. An example of this is when Richard Nixon stated that he did not know about the Watergate break-in and no contradictory information was immediately available. (Eventually, of course, additional information became available to contradict the president's assertions.)

When sources do not agree: When sources do not agree, the analyst will need to choose one or more and declare that this is the view that will be accepted. The historian will need to determine which source is the "better" source. In this case, the term *better* refers to two possible characteristics. A better source is one that:

- Is closer to original documents or oral descriptions, and/or
- Appears more logical or consistent with information outside of any of the sources in dispute.

No matter which source or sources are accepted, it is important to indicate that controversy on the topic exists. The writer should not seem to assure a reader, even by omission, that all sources agree regarding the issue. The rationale for declaring some sources better than others should be made clear.

When one or more sources discuss a topic and another one or more are silent on the topic. One might think that in this situation the historian could simply say that "all sources (that mention the topic) agree," and so believe that the situation happened as described. This is plausible, in some cases, as not all sources will record the same information, and the situation mentioned in one source may simply not have been of much interest to the other source(s). This may be a naïve interpretation of the situation, however, because sometimes sources purposely do not mention aspects of a situation, because they do not want to admit that it occurred. Silence on a topic, in other words, can sometimes be a premeditated lie by omission. The analyst can therefore not rely on silence in a source to indicate that information omitted is unimportant or untrue.

As in most cases of research, a great deal of thought and debate should occur in order to come up with a plausible, if not necessarily perfect, account of the policy being studied.

ADVANTAGES OF THE HISTORICAL APPROACH

The historical approach to studying policy has several advantages. The first, at least for (more or less) current policy analysis, is the sheer amount of source material that is available. Legislative debates, speeches given by key actors during the policy development process, journalistic accounts, memoirs, official documents, regulatory hearings and submissions relating to developing regulations, interviews, and so on, can provide an analyst with an almost overwhelming amount of information relating to the policy and its emergence.

The second advantage is the chronological and straightforward way the information can be presented. First one thing happened, then another, and another, until, finally, the policy emerged. This approach is easy to understand and fits in well with the narrative traditions of Western society.

A final advantage is that of the contextual element. Policies result from needs and tensions in a society created by conditions and events, and related perceptions of and reactions to those conditions and events. Thus, these contextual elements are key in understanding how a policy emerged and how it was subsequently shaped.

CRITIQUES OF THE HISTORICAL APPROACH

Two major criticisms of the historical approach exist. The first is that it is generally descriptive and atheoretical. This means that each case study, while perhaps interesting reading, adds very little to our understanding of larger-scale processes at work. This can be mitigated somewhat by use of multiple case studies with an identical framework to guide the analysis. Blau and Abramovitz (2010), for example, posit five factors as being vital for understanding social policy in the United States (the economy, politics and the structure of government, ideology, social movements, and history) and use this model to describe five social policy areas (income support, jobs and job training, housing, health care, and food and hunger). There is, however, no test of other factors that might be equally (or more) important, no way to ascertain which of these five factors plays a larger part, or if the relative importance changes from one policy arena to another, nor any rationale given for the selection of these five areas.

In addition, the variables (or factors) that are used to explain the policy outcomes are generally not clearly defined, nor are they applied uniformly. We thus have no way of tackling thorny issues relating to how tightly the particular analytical techniques are employed. What is meant, for example, when authors say that "the economy" is an important factor that shapes social policy? How close is the correlation between expansiveness of social policy and, for example, the rate of change of the gross domestic product (or other frequently used variables relating to the size or health of the economy)? And what is the practical implication: does the factor "the economy" affecting social policy mean that social policy is more generous when the economy is booming because there are more resources available to distribute? Or is social policy more generous during times of recession because more people are in need and it is easier to see that one can be out of a job or without money for reasons beyond one's own control? Reasonable arguments can be made on both sides of the economy question.

While quantitative comparative policy analysis is a vibrant field, it is also narrowly circumscribed by variables that can be quantified (budget, staff size, policy outputs or outcomes) and loses what can be called an historical focus. When the historical aspect is included with quantifiable variables, the result is usually still very descriptive. One example of this situation is Gordon's *Social Security Policies in Industrial Countries* (2009). This is a well-received and traditional book on comparative social security systems. Book chapter titles include both descriptive historical elements (e.g., "Postwar Developments" and "National Old Age Pension Programs: Basic Structures") and numerical attributes of different programs (e.g., "Difference in Social Security Spending" and "The Economic Impacts of Pension Programs"). In the end, Gordon's book describes her impressions of what will happen in the future with social security policies, but it has "only" her careful collection of facts and analysis to support her interpretation. As noted earlier, others may use the same facts and come up with different conclusions by approaching the analysis from a different perspective. In addition, Gordon and other quantitative historians tend to ask about the effects of policy in the past, not to try to explain why the particular policy that came about was chosen.

One of the concerns with historical methods is that they are almost always single case studies. A new set of tools is emerging to use qualitative methods comparatively to broaden the extrapolations of findings (i.e., transferring knowledge gained from a policy analysis to analyses of similar situations [Patton, 2002]). Some of the methodologies recently developed include "systematic comparative case study," "qualitative comparative analysis," "fuzzy sets" (Rihoux, 2006), and "meta-synthesis" (Finfgeld, 2003). Methodological problems still exist with these approaches, however, such as overcoming an inherently small number of cases, deciding what "comparable" cases are, selecting appropriate variables, and factoring in potentially different time horizons (Finfgeld-Connett, 2010; Rihoux, 2006). These approaches are promising, but are still in their infancy and face many challenges.

The second major problem for the hermeneutic/interpretive and critical historical approach is the problem faced by qualitative researchers in terms of trustworthiness (a parallel concept to validity and reliability in quantitative research). Strides have been made in developing techniques and descriptions of ways to make qualitative research conclusions less dependent on an individual's singular interpretive capabilities through various types of triangulation (Patton, 2002). Still, researchers of a more positivist leaning find the lack of standardized measures used in qualitative research somewhat disconcerting and unconvincing.

APPLICATION OF THE HISTORICAL APPROACH

We are now ready to apply the historical approach to the creation and passage of the Personal Responsibility and Work Opportunity Reconciliation Act of 1996, using Spano's four questions as a framework. For readers who are not familiar with the welfare reform law and the key actors, this application of the historical approach will also serve as a starting point for future chapters—who did what, when, and where. It will be a condensed version, of course, but it should provide the basic outline, which can then be elaborated upon in later chapters. (A fuller traditional history of the up-close details of the welfare reform legislative process can be found in Haskins [2006]. Haskins was a participant in and observer of the process, working as a high-level staff member of a key committee.)

Identify the relevant actors, their areas of contention, and how they define the problem.

In the mid-1990s, the relevant political actors in the welfare reform debate were numerous. The most obvious ones included Democratic President Bill Clinton, Republican Speaker of the House Newt Gingrich, and Republican Senate Majority Leader Trent Lott. It should be remembered that the Republicans had sent two welfare reform bills to the president that had what he considered extremely harsh provisions. He vetoed both of them, laying out clearly what he saw as the most damaging aspects of the legislation.

While there was considerable agreement on the main issue of requiring welfare recipients to work, there was also great controversy regarding the details. For example, what does it mean to "work"? How many hours per week, over what period of time, counts as "working"? Does attending school count as "working"? Does it matter if the schooling is to obtain a General Educational Development certificate or high school diploma, or attending college classes? Should day care be provided for mothers moving from welfare to work? If not totally paid for by government, how much of the mother's income should go to child care expenses? How long may a recipient maintain eligibility for food stamps and Medicaid? The Republicans (as led by Representative Gingrich and Senator Lott, whom we will treat as "one actor" for the time being) not only wanted to cut the number of welfare recipients, but also wanted to save money and promote their version of morality. Thus, many of the proposals they put forward under the banner of welfare reform touched on welfare only tangentially. The requirement for sex education to be only abstinence-based, for example, did not have a direct connection with the larger topic of reducing dependency; nor did the requirement that faith-based organizations be allowed to compete for government contracts on an equal basis with secular organizations.

The number of topics on which disagreement existed is too large to cover fully in this chapter (see Haskins, 2006, for his much fuller account). Still, the details were important and had the real possibility of derailing the larger policy shift. Senator Lott and Representative Gingrich were not the only actors on the Republican side—they needed to keep their fellow senators and representatives happy and willing to compromise on some issues. Governors of both parties (but especially Republicans) had important input into what the top leaders insisted on. In the summer of 1996, the president's advisors were split on the advisability of signing the third welfare reform bill. Everyone acknowledged that the president had negotiated many improvements in the bill, but there were many areas where the legislation remained imperfect in their eyes, particularly in terms of its treatment of legal immigrants and the possibility of having millions of Americans without any government support after their eligibility ran out.

Just as it is impossible to quickly list all the areas of controversy, so is it impossible to list all the positions of each leader on each issue. In general, however, Republicans wanted to shrink the welfare rolls, save money, and improve the country's morality. Clinton and his advisors wanted to reduce welfare dependency by creating work incentives, but do so in a way that provided many social services (such as day care and job training) to improve the lives of former recipients. Democrats believed that Republicans merely wanted to cut AFDC expenditures and had little interest in future of the former recipients; Republicans were skeptical that Democrats were committed to making recipients become more accountable for making their own living.

Examine sources to try to understand why the issue is being considered at that particular time in history. Determine if it is a new problem and what specific events may have sparked the policy debate.

The Aid to Dependent Children (later renamed "Aid to Families with Dependent Children") program was the program informally known as "welfare." Written as Title IV of the original 1935 Social Security Act, the program was initially conceived of as a way to assist fatherless children and their mothers. The general assumption was that the parents would have been married and that the father would have died. The ADC program was seen as a small and stopgap program, to be needed only until the survivor's benefits portion of the Social Security legislation had a chance to mature.

In the mid-1930s, most mothers stayed at home while fathers supported the family through farming or outside work. The ADC program was modeled on state-level programs known as "mothers' pensions," which provided small amounts of cash support to women and their children who, through no fault of their own, were without a primary breadwinner in the household. In general, although the ADC program was aimed at children whose father had died, the program also paid cash to children whose father had abandoned the family. Legislators believed it was better to keep the remainder of the family together than to force the mother to turn the care of her children over to the state entirely, by putting them into an orphanage.

By the late 1960s, however, the nature of the AFDC program had changed. The program had grown in numbers of recipients. In 1962, about 3.5 million Americans were receiving AFDC benefits. This increased rapidly to around five million recipients just five years later, in 1967. The reasons for the increase included:

- expanded rules, providing for greater numbers of people being eligible;
- the migration of African Americans to cities, where they were more likely to receive assistance than in their previous Southern and rural homes;

- the increasing divorce rate;
- the increasing rate of children being born out of wedlock;
- the improved ability of community action groups to help eligible families receive assistance; and
- the changing views regarding women and work.

This last point had several effects. First, as more "never-married" women had children and applied for AFDC benefits, the notion of the recipients' being deserving of assistance eroded. Second, more women were working outside the home, so it was increasingly difficult to support the idea that poor women should stay at home to care for their children. Also, as the proportion of African American women in the program increased, political opposition to the program increased based on underlying negative racial attitudes by whites regarding blacks.

Prior to the early 1990s, other efforts had been made to alter the welfare system. President Nixon, spurred by Senator Daniel Patrick Moynihan, made an effort to develop a guaranteed income program, called the Family Assistance Plan. Although work requirements were included in this proposal, mothers of preschool children were to be exempt from working (Nixon, 1969). The legislative effort was stymied by mistrust of the president and a relatively low level of proposed financial aid, which eliminated most support by liberals in Congress (Burke and Burke, 1974). In the wake of this defeat, AFDC rolls increased to nearly 11 million people by the mid-1970s, and food stamp recipients skyrocketed from about one million to 19 million recipients (Danziger, 1999). Costs rose substantially as well, and, because of the amount of income that was deducted from the welfare benefits of recipients who found employment, work was not a rational option for many of the poor. This led critics such as Martin Anderson (1978) and Charles Murray (1984) to spread their message that the expanded programs were evidence of a deleterious dependency on government-run programs by a class of citizens who would never be able to fend for themselves unless welfare was eliminated.

A few years later, President Carter also tried to change the AFDC program. His proposal, the Program for Better Jobs and Income (PBJI), would have guaranteed an income and a job to every welfare recipient (Danziger, 1999). This program would have increased the number of welfare recipients; would have linked receipt of benefits to work expectations, other than for mothers of preschool-aged children; and would have been tremendously expensive, probably the most important reason it was not enacted into law (Danziger, 1999). PBJI was the first important welfare reform proposal that would have decreased the amount of benefits given to someone who was expected to work but who chose not to, including not working in a government-funded job of last resort (Danziger, 1999).

The third major welfare reform initiative (and the only one to pass Congress to be signed into law) was the Family Support Act of 1988 (FSA). It was supported by both liberals and conservatives (Baum, 1991; Danziger, 1999; Haskins, 1991; and Mead, 1992). One of the provisions of the FSA was that clients were expected to work more than previous policy had required (including mothers of children older than three years), which pleased conservatives. There were also sanctions in place for recipients who did not participate in the jobs training program. Offsetting these provisions, in the minds of liberals, was that states were required to broaden eligibility requirements and to provide services to make the transition to work successful, such as basic skills training, job placement services, day care, and transportation. These work and support requirements were enacted shortly before a recession hit the United States. Partially in response to that, the AFDC-UP (Unemployed Parent) program was passed in 1990. In this program, states were required to provide benefits to low-income families that included two parents, thus reducing the problem of fathers' needing to leave their home in order for their children and the children's mother to become eligible for AFDC payments. Primarily because of the recession, welfare rolls grew from about 11 million to 14 million people, setting the stage for increased concern regarding welfare costs and the dependency of some people on government handouts.

Thus, the history of welfare reform efforts can be said to have started in the late 1960s, as AFDC rolls and costs increased. As American society changed, conservative critics became more likely to blame government programs for increases in divorce rates, illegitimate births, and dependence on government benefits. By the early 1990s, there were few supporters of the idea of keeping AFDC the way it was, but there was considerable disagreement about the types of changes that would be beneficial (Haskins, 2006).

In addition, the timing of the issue was related to the electoral cycle. Bill Clinton, starting when he was governor of Arkansas, had a long history of trying to improve the workings of welfare. When he ran for president in 1992, he had promised to "end welfare as we know it." In his first two years in office, he had not moved forward with efforts to change welfare, even though he had a Democratic majority in the Senate and the House. In the 1994 midterm elections, the Republicans, led by Newt Gingrich and influenced by his Contract with America, had taken over both chambers of Congress. One of the elements of the Contract with America was welfare reform. Congress passed two welfare reform bills between 1994 and 1996, but the president vetoed both of them because he considered them too punitive to welfare recipients. Thus, in the summer before the 1996 elections, both President Clinton and the Republicans had reason to bring up the issue to try to achieve their campaign promises.

Discern the ideology behind the policy positions.

There was a clear difference in ideology on most of the issues contained in welfare reform. For Republicans, welfare reform was Point 3 of the Contract with American, stating:

> THE PERSONAL RESPONSIBILITY ACT: Discourage illegitimacy and teen pregnancy by prohibiting welfare to minor mothers and denying increased AFDC for additional children while on welfare, cut spending for welfare programs, and enact a tough two-years-and-out provision with work requirements to promote individual responsibility (United States House of Representatives, 1994).

Democrats, on the other hand, were torn between defending the status quo against those on the right who wanted to dismantle it entirely, and advocating the idea that a humane overhaul of the welfare system was needed. One example of such an overhaul was called the Democratic Work First Plan. According to Al From, president of the Democratic Leadership Council (DLC) in 1996, The Democratic Work First Plan:

> . . . would make cash welfare payments temporary and contingent on rapid movement toward full-time, unsubsidized work.

> It abolishes the two big and ineffective welfare programs—AFDC and JOBS—and replaces them with a streamlined system that rewards states

for placing welfare recipients in real jobs and keeping them there. States would have nearly as much flexibility as in a block grant, but would be held accountable for results, earning performance bonuses if they succeed in placing and keeping recipients in jobs, and suffering sanctions if they don't (From, 1996).

To look at the two political parties' positions on a specific topic within the larger debate, let us examine the issue of protecting children. Republicans believed that the best way for the government to assist children was to require their parents to take financial responsibility for them, including paying child support if both parents were not in the child's home, and working at a job. The discipline of work would help mothers enforce discipline on their children and offer a good role model for the future. Republicans also believed that income from a job would be higher than the benefits provided by the government and that this would be good for children (Haskins, 2006).

Democrats, on the other hand, citing evidence from an Urban Institute study, believed that children would be harmed by the provisions of the Republican welfare reform efforts. Over a million children would be thrown into poverty because of the Republicans' insistence on time limits for receiving benefits, the potential difficulty for adult recipients to find and keep work, and the "work-first" approach to getting a job. Little funding was provided for skills training and job supports that Democrats considered necessities if mothers were expected to find and keep work. In addition, there was no guarantee that income from work (particularly at a minimum-wage job) would equal the benefit package of government programs. Thus, far from being beneficial for children, welfare reform in the Republican mode would be detrimental.

Democrats also were keeping faith with their principles of providing a broader and more generous welfare state. Democrats were the instigators of the welfare state in America and its expansion since 1935. Unemployment insurance, food stamps, Medicare, Medicaid, and most other programs to provide assistance to the poor and unemployed were the direct result of efforts Democrats had made, usually over fierce opposition from Republicans. Constituencies for Democratic officeholders did not want to see welfare programs dismantled.

Welfare policy and welfare reform showed stark differences between conservatives and liberals. Middle ground was limited and difficult to identify in this situation. Republicans in Congress had passed two different welfare reform bills that President Clinton vetoed because he considered them too harsh. The third bill to come to his desk, in the summer of 1996, was somewhat better from his perspective, but was still objectionable.

Try to identify similarities and differences in the political context between the social policy conflict under study and previous efforts to address the topic. What may have led to the resurgence of policy debate regarding this topic?

Let us choose for comparison the three major reforms discussed earlier: President Nixon's Family Assistance Plan, President Carter's Program for Better Jobs and Income, and the situation President Clinton found himself in.

Nixon, working with one of the most knowledgeable and respected Democratic Senators, Senator Daniel Patrick Moynihan, with a long history of work on welfare issues, tried to make changes to welfare at the end of the turbulent 1960s. His proposal surprised many Democrats, who had control of both Houses of Congress. In order for his plan to succeed, he was required to work across the aisle and fashion a coalition of moderate Republicans and Democrats. In the end, conservative Republicans who would never pass a guaranteed income program such as the FAP, and liberal Democrats, who disliked the low level of guaranteed income proposed (which was necessary to get even the slight Republican support that was achieved), killed the bill (Burke and Burke, 1974).

Democratic President Carter faced a different situation in that Democrats controlled both houses of Congress during his time in office. Thus, the assumption would be that his proposals would face an easy time. Yet, it was not to be. Jimmy Carter ran as an outsider to the tainted problems of Washington, D.C., and was the first elected president after Richard Nixon's Watergate scandal and resignation. He won election over Gerald Ford, Nixon's vice-president, who took office upon Nixon's resignation. But it was a narrow victory, with Carter receiving only 50.1% of the vote, and just 297 Electoral College votes compared to Ford's 240. Carter brought in a cadre of trusted people from Georgia, where he had been governor, and did not know how to use his position to influence members of his own party in Congress, many of whom did not owe their elections to his popularity. Thus, his lack of political skill was part of the situation in the late 1970s. Carter also was president when the country faced an energy shortage brought on by an oil embargo by oil-producing countries, high unemployment, a recession, the attack on the U.S. Embassy in Iran, with Americans held hostage for months, and a failed rescue attempt to free them. When he left office, 55% of Americans disapproved of his handling of his job (Gallop poll, 2009).

The situation for Bill Clinton started well when he was elected, as he had a majority of Democrats in the Senate and the House of Representatives. Instead of using the first two years of his term to push welfare reform, however, he chose to tackle health care reform, an effort that was eventually defeated and served as a rallying point for Republican opposition to government programs more generally. Republican efforts to criticize government and Democrats worked well, and they took control of the Senate and the House in the 1994 midterm elections. Newly chosen Republican Speaker of the House Newt Gingrich had created a much more partisan era and used the Contract with America to emphasize the differences between the two parties. Clinton found himself without a significant legislative achievement on a signature issue, welfare reform, moving into the 1996 presidential election and facing a hostile Congress.

The answer to the question, "Why did TANF pass in the form it did?" relates to voter anger over health care reform efforts by the president, which Republicans capitalized on to win a majority in the House and Senate. With their new majorities, they had the president, who was actually partially in agreement with them, in a tough spot. He had promised in his campaigning to bring forth a new welfare system and he needed to do so. The timing was correct, the actors were in place, and so everything worked out to have this bill be passed and signed.

STRENGTHS AND WEAKNESSES OF THE HISTORICAL APPROACH

The historical approach is perhaps the most common type of policy analysis found in social work policy textbooks. Popple and Leighninger (2008, p. 71) argue that "History . . . helps us understand and deal with current policies. It gives us some sense of the context of how and why particular programs and approaches developed and how well they achieved what they set out to do." They caution, however, that this analysis works best if the policy historian has a guiding framework to the analysis. Other authors (Blau and Abramovitz, 2010; Chambers and Wedel, 2008; Karger and Stoesz, 2010) also support the idea that understanding the history of a policy is helpful in understanding current policy. Other authors do not highlight historical analysis in their policy texts (Ambrosino et al., 2008; Barusch, 2006; DiNitto and Cummins, 2007).

Historical policy analysis is usually a qualitative approach, featuring interviews with key players, if they still are alive, and combing the historical record in search of sources. Almost all standard social work policy analysts adopt a very descriptive approach to their material, and few do the type of in-depth use of primary source documents that "true" historians espouse. A few impose a thematic filter on their books (Blau and Abramovitz, 2010; and Day, 2008, are good examples of this) but most introductory social history and policy texts follow a conventional descriptive approach to their historical analysis and their writing on current policy.

The strengths of the historical approach are that it is easy to understand, focuses on the context of the policy's existence over time, and, when done thematically, it can provide the reader with useful (though perhaps controversial) perspectives on the bare facts. Contextual elements, specifically, are useful in extrapolation.

The weaknesses of the historical approach include the difficulties in extrapolation of interpretation, the difficulty in finding and using primary sources for many historical periods, and the overwhelming amount of information on recent policies. The lack of quantification and the difficulty in testing hypotheses statistically can be seen as weaknesses as well. As noted above, without a clear framework to help the reader understand the bare facts, it is possible to learn all the dates and actors without having much understanding of the meaning. It can be as dry as knowing that the Personal Responsibility and Work Opportunities Act was signed on August 22, 1996. Knowing that one fact (and even adding hundreds more such facts) provides little in the way of knowing what, why, and how the most important legislation regarding income support in 60 years became law.

Historical policy analysis can sometimes lead to the feeling that the outcome was inevitable—that, given what had come before, and who the leaders were at that time, no other results were possible. This type of deterministic reading of history is problematic because of the large number of variables that could have caused large differences in policy outcomes.

3

Using the Politics and Power Approach

Studying policy through the lenses of politics and power analysis is an approach that focuses on who wins and who loses, based on their relative power resources at different points in the policy process. Introducing a policy process model combined with differential power analysis, this chapter provides readers a way of understanding policy through looking at how influence, persuasion, and decision making are conducted by system insiders and those who want to be on the inside. A discussion of elitist and pluralistic approaches to understanding policy decisions is included as background to the analysis of TANF. These theories are important in that they describe the relative weight of "the people" in the thinking of decision makers.

DESCRIPTION OF THE POLITICS AND POWER APPROACH, INCLUDING PLURALISM AND ELITISM

One of the primary questions in the study of policy making is, "Who decides?" (Compare this with the title of a highly influential book by Dahl [1961], *Who Governs?*) One view is that those with power resources, particularly money, are the ones who decide what government policy becomes. But financial resources are only one source of power, and it is important to look at a broader range of possible sources of power. A second major question in understanding how policy is created is, "What is power?"

Power has been compared to "oxygen in the bloodstream" (Hudson and Lowe, 2009, p. 112) and "electrical current," because we cannot see it, yet having it or not is vital to making things happen. Power is the ability to get things done. Dahl's famous definition is "A has power over B to the extent that he can get B to do something that B would not otherwise do" (Dahl, 1957, pp. 202–203). One reason for policy to be designed in a particular way, then, is because one actor, with sufficient power, gets other actors to go along with that proposal. This could be considered an *active* use of power, getting something done. Allen (2005) notes that this conception of power is "*power over*" someone. A second use of power is to keep a proposal from being adopted or considered. Bachrach and Baratz (1962) termed this the "second face" of power—the power to stop consideration of a policy, or, at a more hidden level, the power to keep an idea from even coming up in people's minds as a realistic option. Suppose, for example, that someone proposed to eliminate capitalism in the United States. The idea would not be considered as reasonable at all, because the social and political values and institutions of the United States are so intertwined with the economic system of capitalism that the proposal would mean, in effect, starting over. Thus this idea of drastically revising the economic system in the United States is hardly ever mentioned, even when economic crisis exists and affects millions of Americans.

One of the next important questions in understanding social policy formation is to ask what the distribution of power is in a particular situation. This may be considered a different approach to understanding power; in Allen's (2005) words, it is the "*power to*" accomplish something. Thus power can be seen as a resource that is unequally distributed along various lines. An individual's power can be the result of his or her position in an institution or organization (institutional power). Individuals in key positions are the players in any particular policy decision. The president of the United States, for example, has the power to command the armed forces of the country as a constitutional right. (This example shows how the concepts of *power to* and *power over* can be wielded by the same person.). But the power (or lack of power) in a specific job is only its potential. Individuals have their own strengths, weaknesses, interests, and commitments that affect the nominal power of their positions. Power can be gained by bargaining or leveraging personal ties, bluffing, skillfully using resources or other situations (situational power). Congresswoman A may vote for Congressman B's proposal now, in exchange for a promise from Congressman B to support her with a future vote or money for her reelection campaign. A policy actor may feel loyalty to another person and so provide support in almost all cases. Institutional power remains fairly constant; situational power will vary from one individual to another and even then can change quickly. This fluctuation can be due to a number of factors, including who else chooses to be involved, attention span, crises considered more immediate or pressing, and even the actor's health status. A personal scandal can weaken an actor's power position very quickly, even forcing the person from office. When this happens, both the person's situational and institutional powers evaporate.

We can talk about the distribution of power on a larger scale, as well. To what extent are the citizens of a country in charge of policy, and how does government respond to the differing desires of individuals, organizations, and groups in society? We will discuss two theories about these questions, pluralism and elitism.

PLURALISM

Pluralism posits that there are multiple centers of power in the country and that government is a fairly neutral arbiter of the relative power of groups active in a particular policy question. "Pluralist theories explain how conflict between a wide range of actors shapes policy. That is why they seem a sensible place to start thinking about policy-making. . . ." (Ney, 2009, p. 195). The people of the nation, when they desire to do so, band together into interest groups to try to affect policy matters. These groups may be temporary, like a citizen's group to stop undesired development in its neighborhood; or more organized and permanent, such as a business lobby, the National Association of Manufacturers (NAM) (www.nam.org) or the National Small Business Association (NSBA) (www.nsba.biz); a professional lobby, the National Association of Social Workers (NASW) (www.socialworkers.org) or the American Trial

Lawyer's Association (www.theatla.org); or an interest-based lobby, like the American Association of Retired Persons (AARP) (www.aarp.org) or the American Philatelic Society (APS) (www.stamps.org). In a pluralistic democracy, overlapping organizational memberships are considered good. Thus, a member of one group may be a member of other groups as well: a small business–owning social worker over the age of 60 who collects stamps may be a member of the NSBA, NASW, AARP, and APS! Sometimes these groups will be on the same side of a debate, and sometimes they will be on different sides. One can easily imagine, for example, that AARP and NASW agree that Medicare and Social Security funding should be strengthened. In another case, the small business–owner's association might come out against mandatory health care coverage at one's place of employment, while the National Association of Social Workers considers this a positive policy. Also, each organization's allies may change, depending on the issue. While interest groups tend to keep the same allies time after time, there is still some fluidity from one debate to another.

From the perspective of pluralist democracy, such overlapping memberships and changing alliances are considered positive because it means that people will not wish to completely "destroy" their adversaries in one policy battle because those current opponents may be needed to lend support on the next issue. To use a sports analogy, if you know you may be traded to another team next week, you do not have an incentive to injure the players on that team this week. You play hard, because you want to win, but you follow the rules as enforced by an umpire or other disinterested official. Pluralism, with overlapping interest-group memberships and a government keeping everyone honest in the policy-making process, thus encourages a considerable amount of moderation in debate and policy making.

If the situation were that people were always in mutually exclusive and never-changing groups, there would be a tendency to move towards extremism, as in ethnic or religious strife. The movement away from bipartisanship in the American political debate and in Congress has led to increasingly strident elections and policy decisions at the national level. Compromise is difficult if you consider your opponent "evil" or "corrupt."

The relative power of each of the actors in a policy contest varies from issue to issue and case to case. While Dahl (1961), one of the foremost thinkers regarding pluralism, believed that all groups in American had at least latent power, due to their ability to organize, he did not believe that all groups were equal in power. Wealthy persons and business organizations are frequently seen to have better access to decision makers, due to campaign contributions or to their economic impact on a constituency. But these individuals and groups are not all-powerful for two reasons. First, they do not always agree on issues amongst themselves. Secondly, countervailing resources exist that other groups may possess, such as a labor union with large numbers of politically active members. Some groups may acquire influence due to their special knowledge or their skills to persuade policy makers based on the merit of their arguments.

The role of government in the pluralist version of society is to act as a relatively neutral referee, to enforce the rules of fair play, including the obligation of organizations and groups to engage in negotiation with each other to come to an acceptable outcome. The structures of government should also reflect competing and independent centers of power. Thus, as in the American Constitution, a separation of powers between legislative, executive, and judicial centers should be created, and each of the branches of government should have the ability to limit the other branches' ability to enact policy (this is the concept of "checks and balances"). The legislative body, Congress, is itself divided into a longer-serving Senate, where each state has equal representation, and the shorter-term House of Representatives, where each member represents an approximately equal number of people.

Thus, the president may veto legislation passed by Congress, although Congress may override the president's veto if a large majority (two-thirds of the voting members of each chamber) in both the Senate and the House vote in favor of the legislation. Similarly, the Supreme Court can declare a law unconstitutional, or order the executive branch to cease an activity, while the president appoints justices and judges to fill vacancies (with the consent of the Senate), and the Congress may impeach and remove a sitting member of the judicial branch.

The American system is also organized according the principle of "federalism," in that the national government has certain constitutionally delegated responsibilities and the states have the rest. National defense, for example, is a responsibility of the federal government, although each state also has National Guard units. The National Guard dates to colonial militias, and answer to "both the president of the United States and the governors of their respective states and territories" (www.nationalguard.com). The federal government is also tasked with regulating the trade that occurs between people in different states, and in taxing imports into and exports from the United States.

Federalism also allows states to have separate laws concerning education, health, criminal justice, and social welfare policy (among others), because these are primarily the responsibility of states. States have the ability to create smaller units of government, such as counties and cities, as well as special-use government bodies such as school or water conservation districts.

A related aspect to the separation of powers and checks and balances between the branches of government is that organizations wishing to impact policy have many options regarding where their influence may be felt. If the United States Congress seems filled with legislators unfriendly to their cause, advocates may seek to move to the judicial system to receive a favorable Supreme Court decision. If the entire federal system is not willing to move forward in a particular way, an organization may decide to exert its effort at the state level. Opponents of abortion rights, for example, finding that the Supreme Court would not reverse the decision in Roe v. Wade, have moved to have laws passed at the state level that limit the right to an abortion in various ways, while also working with various presidents to appoint Supreme Court justices who are willing to consider overturning the decision in question.

In summary, pluralists argue that power is spread throughout society and that government acts primarily as a referee to reflect public opinion fairly, through a peaceful (though often contentious) process. In the American case, pluralism is built into the institutions of government through separation of powers between the branches and between the two chambers of Congress, as well as by checks and balances between the branches and, finally, through federalism, the separation of power between the national government and state governments.

CRITIQUE OF PLURALISM

The pluralist position on the (relatively) widespread dispersion of power or potential power has been challenged on many fronts. Some of the challenges are based on an oversimplification of the pluralist position. Pluralists do not, for example, believe that power is distributed evenly across all types of people or all varieties of interests. That is clearly not true. Some people and groups are more active (sometimes for systematic reasons) and those who are active have greater success in promoting their ideas than those who are not. Systematic reasons include overt repression (poll taxes and literacy tests are two examples of methods used in the past), and more or less subtle dissuasion (when whole groups of people do not receive information on how to participate effectively, or are given incorrect information in an effort to prevent participation, or when some people are slandered or called, for example, Communists or troublemakers in a concerted effort to prevent their participation). Pluralists take into account these problems of equality and involvement and agree that the system needs to be made even fairer than it currently is, but they also maintain that, compared to most places in the world, the American system is amazingly open.

A more trenchant critique of pluralism is that it ignores the ability of some actors to control the agenda   that is, the issues that come to the fore for public discussion and debate. As noted earlier, Bachrach and Baratz (1962) called the ability to prevent a topic from being discussed as the "second face" of power. If some topics are "off limits" to even consider, they argue, then power is being exerted to keep the public from learning about potentially contentious issues. If this occurs, then policy conversations are merely about topics of relative unimportance, and the puppet-masters are firmly in control of society.

ELITISM

The question is, "Who is so capable in using the second face of power?" This brings in a major challenger to the ideas of pluralism: the theory of elite power, or *elitism*. This has both stronger and weaker positions. A strong position (as in Marxism) suggests that the economic elite is in control of not just the economy, but of almost all aspects of policy. Power is concentrated into a few hands, the hands of the wealthiest members of society. Government is not a neutral arbiter between groups in society— government is controlled by and therefore on the side of the oppressors. In the Marxist view, the capitalist system is unable to be reformed.

Therefore it is necessary to foment revolution and completely eliminate the current way of governing. Once this is accomplished, power will be more equally shared among members of the working class, who will be self-governing.

A weaker version of elitism is sometimes called the *plural elite* model. In this view, there are a few different sets of elites, with differing views, who use their wealth and influence to compete for additional power. The groups use their control of the media to woo members of the middle and working classes to support their proposals and views. Government is biased in favor of the elites, but nonetheless takes into account the wishes of the other classes in order to maintain its power base.

All three views of the distribution of power in the United States (pluralism, strong elitism, and plural elitism) have evidence in their support, yet it may be said that the plural elite model is most highly supported. The majority of people eligible to vote do not do so, at least not in most elections. Still, large swings in voting can be attributed to issues being raised and identified with particular candidates. The Barack Obama presidential campaign in 2008, for example, brought into the political process large numbers of African Americans who were enthusiastic about being able to vote for him.

INFORMATION NEEDED TO USE THE POLITICS AND POWER APPROACH

According to Allison and Zelikow (1999), four questions should be answered to use what they term "Model III":

1. *Who* plays? That is, whose views and values count in shaping the choice and action?
2. What *factors* shape each *player's* (a) perceptions; (b) preferred course of action; and thus (c) the player's stand on the issue?
3. What *factors* account for each player's impact on the choice and action?
4. What is the *"action channel,"* that is, the established process for aggregating competing perceptions, preferences, and stands of players in making decisions and taking action? (emphases in original, p. 390)

ADVANTAGES OF THE POLITICS AND POWER APPROACH

The major advantage of the politics and power approach is that it provides a great deal of conceptual understanding and detail about the necessity of bargaining to reach decisions within government, even by officials who have considerably more power than others. The president, the Speaker of the House, and the Senate majority leader must bargain with each other and with many other participants. Haskins (2006) makes the point in his detailed history that welfare reform could have foundered many times due to disputes among Republican senators, representatives, governors, and staff. Every chapter of his book provides examples of the challenges faced by the Speaker to get the bill passed in a form that President Clinton might sign. Government action is thus the result of group processes: different actors "pulling in different directions produce a result . . . distinct from what any person or group intended" (Allison and Zelikow, 1999, p. 256). This is as true within the White House as in Congress (Allison and Zelikow, 1999).

By stating this assumption as a central tenet of the model, and attending to the ramifications of it, the analyst understands the situation in much the same way as the participants do. When firsthand accounts of policy decisions are read (such as those on welfare reform by Haskins, 2006, and Lott, 1995), a great deal of time is spent describing the main actors, their positions, and the bargaining sessions (formal and informal) that took place. Thus, the primary advantage of the model is that it seems to be the way things actually happen.

One might read this chapter and think that the politics and power model presented here is simply a more detailed version of the historical approach presented in the previous chapter. The key difference between this model and the historical model, however, is the explicit focus on the actors' positions, their decision-making processes, and the politics of bargaining. The questions asked in the two types of analysis are not the same, and thus one does not emerge with the same answers. While the two models start at similar places (who the key actors are and what their positions are), the historical model pays much more attention to the longer view. It attempts to place the policy in a larger context, which includes the context of ideology, the sweep of time, and comparisons between past and present. The politics and power model is much more focused on a "thick description" of the actors' strengths and strategies, the twists and turns of bargaining between them, and the outcomes that emerge from this process.

CRITIQUES OF THE POLITICS AND POWER APPROACH

For all the benefit of the politics and power approach, we may rightly ask the purpose of undertaking such an extensive look at the way policy is made. Are the answers we derive really that much more valuable than what a typical historical analysis provides? Or that the rational actor approach (see the next chapter) gives? The information needed to answer the questions is greater, the time to gather the information is longer, and the ability to generalize from the analysis is no greater than by using the other two approaches.

As is true of most things, the purpose of the endeavor needs to dominate the methods chosen. So, if the research question of a study demands to know the strategies of the individuals and the inner workings of groups involved in a decision, the politics and power model is very appropriate. Otherwise, there may not be a good reason to undertake the strenuous efforts needed to do the job sufficiently well to be of use.

USING THE POLITICS AND POWER APPROACH

Using the four questions posed by Allison and Zelikow (1999) noted earlier as a framework for this application section, let us analyze the passage of the Personal Responsibility and Work Opportunities Reconciliation Act of 1996.

Who plays? That is, whose views and values count in shaping the choice and action?

According to several biographies of Bill Clinton and histories of the welfare reform debates, the most important players in the welfare reform process were President Bill Clinton and Speaker of the House Newt Gingrich. Senate Majority Leader Trent Lott was also essential in deliberations. Their positions made them the obvious key actors. Their personalities had an effect, of course, and in some ways insured that

Senator Lott was less important than President Clinton and Speaker Gingrich. Newt Gingrich might even be considered the most influential person in bringing the welfare reform issue to a head, as he had included it as a major feature of the Contract with America, a policy initiative that received considerable attention in the election of Republicans to Congress. Other actors were important as well, however.

At least two of the most important voices working within the administration had no official government position. First Lady Hillary Rodham Clinton was a strong force in the administration and was a close advisor to the president on most policy issues. John Harris (2005) discusses her role in the debate by noting her absence from a meeting held to decide if President Clinton should sign the Republican welfare reform bill or not:

> The most influential advisor was absent from the meeting entirely. Since the health care debacle, Hillary Clinton typically did not appear at White House deliberations like this one. No one doubted that the views of the first lady, a longtime policy advocate for poor children, were being heard. . . . Hillary Clinton's aides and friends believed that privately she was keeping up the pressure on her husband but it became obvious that her own view was softening (pp. 237–238).

A second actor who had no official position in government was Dick Morris, the president's major political advisor and pollster. Morris had advised Clinton to enact the most popular parts of the Republicans' Contract with America, such as welfare reform, in some fashion so as to reduce the chances for Republicans to continue to use those issues against the Democrats. Morris urged the president to sign the bill. "Welfare veto would be a disaster," and would probably cost the president his chance for a second term in the upcoming election against Republican candidate Bob Dole (Harris, 2005, p. 232). An interesting connection between Senator Lott and President Clinton was that they both used Dick Morris as their trusted political advisor, a fact that was an irritant to many liberal Democrats inside the White House and out (Gillon, 2008; Lott, 2005). Dick Morris became the conduit for negotiations and agreements between the senator and the White House that, while sometimes contentious, served the interests of both. Without this linkage, it is possible that the Personal Responsibility and Work Opportunities Act of 1996 would not have emerged at all, and certainly not in the form it did.

Many other people were involved in the decision-making process within the White House due to both their positions and their personalities. One such person was a policy aide named Bruce Reed who had helped write the speech Clinton gave to announce that he was running for president. His main job was to be the link between the White House and moderate Democrats in Congress and, in the end, provide the most compelling reasons for the president to sign the third welfare reform act sent to him by Congress (Blumenthal, 2003; Gillon, 2008; Harris, 2005; Haskins, 2006). According to Harris (2005, p. 235):

> In the summer of 1996, he [Reed] was one of the few supporters of enacting welfare reform who could speak to the policy side of Clinton's mind. Reed's job was to serve as the president's intellectual lifeline each time he was swept by new doubts. . . . At such moments, Reed would try to untangle the hyperbolic assertions of liberal critics, and remind him of the improvements (more money for child care, for instance) that the administration had managed to wrest from Republicans.

Cabinet members such as Health and Human Services Secretary Donna Shalala, Labor Secretary Robert Reich, Treasury Secretary Robert Rubin, and Housing Secretary Henry Cisneros were all in favor of vetoing the bill. So was Chief of Staff Leon Panetta. Other high-level advisors were in favor of signing the bill. This group included Vice-President Al Gore, Commerce Secretary Mickey Kantor, and White House aide Rahm Emanuel.

Activists from outside the White House also tried to influence the president's position. Marion Wright Edelman, for example, leader of the Children's Defense Fund, and friend of Hillary Clinton, who sat on the board of directors of the Children's Defense Fund, was vehemently against the Republicans' plan, arguing that it would be highly deleterious to the well-being of children in low-income families. Other Democratic constituencies, such as the National Organization of Women and the National Council of La Raza also expressed outrage over the president's willingness to sign the legislation (Vobeja and Balz, 1996). One critic of the Republican position alleged that passing the bill would lead to large numbers of people becoming both homeless and starving within four years (Mandell, 1995).

The most important actors on the Republican side were the Senate majority leader, Senator Trent Lott, from Mississippi; and the Speaker of the House, Representative Newt Gingrich of Georgia. Of these two, Senator Lott was clearly the less important for most of the time negotiations were taking place, at least according to several Clinton biographies (Gillon, 2008; Hamilton, 2007; Harris, 2005). But Senator Lott was also indispensable because no welfare reform bill was going to be passed without his support.

These were the decision-makers at the "micro" level—the deciders who had the biggest say. But we need to examine the possibility that the reason the decision makers in Congress and the White House wanted to reform welfare in the first place was to go along with the desires of the public or a larger elite system. If this is true, then we perhaps have support for one of these two ways of understanding policy making.

Pluralism. A great deal of opinion polling on the subject of welfare reform was conducted in the years of welfare reform debates. From January 1, 1994, to March 25, 1995, for example, Paden and Page (2003) found 542 survey questions that were asked by polling organizations, with large numbers of national and state or regional newspapers providing coverage of the topic before passage of the bill. Sometimes general questions were asked, but other times very specific questions were used. An example of the latter type of question was when respondents were asked if they preferred five-year or two-year lifetime eligibility limits for those on welfare. According to Paden and Page (2003, p. 672), "The poll data were sufficient to offer some concrete policy guidance to any decision-maker who might seek it."

In summarizing their findings, Paden and Page (2003, p. 676–677) stated:

> All-in-all, our findings suggest a marked lack of respect by elected public officials for survey research concerning public opinion on policy issues. These findings are likely to be discouraging to many proponents of democratic theory who believe that elected representatives should pay close attention to the best available evidence about what policies the citizens want them to enact.

Elitism. An alternative view, that the putative decision makers were following the dictates of economic elites, has also been put forward. Abramovitz (2006) believes that every president since Ronald Reagan (1980 and onward) has wanted the same basic laissez-faire economic policies that benefit large business interests. In an era of increased global competition, companies in China, Indonesia, Vietnam, Mexico, El Salvador, and elsewhere make products cheaply, providing low wages and few or no benefits to their workers. American companies were not able to compete profitably under laws and union contracts requiring job benefits and taxes to support needed government social welfare programs to cushion unemployment and other problems of capitalism. Thus, the underlying policy environment was shaped in a way to allow American companies (or, more accurately, multi-national businesses based in the United States) to increase their profits. Per Abramovitz, the four goals of the "elite consensus" are to (1) lower the cost of labor; (2) shrink the welfare state; (3) limit the role of the federal government; and (4) weaken the political influence of social movements (2006, p. 26). These goals use the following policy prescriptions: (1) have taxes that are lower and less progressive; (2) fund social programs at lower levels; (3) move responsibility for social programs from the federal government level to state government level (devolution); and (4) privatize social welfare responsibilities by moving them from the public sector (government) to the private charitable sector (Abramovitz, p. 27) (for more on this line of thinking, see Reisch and Gorin, 2000). Abramovitz and others with a similar perspective (e.g., Joseph, 2006; Reisch, 2006) further argue that welfare reform was part of a larger ideological assault on equal rights for women and for racial minorities. Kilty and Segal (2006) concur: "Bill Clinton and far too many Democrats played into this process, but it was an assault led by conservative Republicans" (p. 1). This group of Republicans and their financial backers certainly could be considered an "elite" with considerable power to create policy and thus have power over vulnerable populations such as women, minorities, and immigrants. Such policies would benefit wealthy white males.

Despite the conclusion that political power in the United States lies only in the hands of a power elite, many of the same authors who argue that welfare reform was part of the overall progress toward a neo-liberal (if not entirely libertarian) state also remind readers that social movements and social actions can have a positive effect in maintaining social justice (Abramovitz, 2006; Joseph, 2006; Nelson, 2006). This undercuts the claim that all power is in the hands of a few. If it were, there would be no point to engaging in a political struggle for increased human rights and greater equality.

In addition, it very much matters who is in the particular micro-level decision-making roles. Bill Clinton, vilified as he is by some, did not sign the first two welfare reform bills sent to him by Congress, as former Republican President George H. W. Bush probably would have done, had he been reelected to the presidency. The election of Barack Obama to the presidency of the United States permitted the passage of far-reaching health care reform. Such legislation probably would not even have been introduced had the Republican ticket of Senator John McCain and Governor Sarah Palin been elected instead.

Let us now turn to the second question to be answered when using the politics and power model, and focus on the individual decision-makers involved in the decisions about welfare reform; notably, President Clinton, Speaker Gingrich, and Senator Lott.

What *factors* shape each *player's* perceptions, preferred course of action, and thus the player's stand on the issue?

Let us look primarily at the three key players as we answer these questions. President Clinton, Senator Lott, and Speaker Gingrich, each of whom had a large impact on the final legislation.

President Clinton. President Clinton, as a former governor, had a view of the world that included what it was like to deal with issues at the state level, including welfare and the AFDC program specifically. His perceptions were thus firmly rooted in experiences of being responsible for implementing policy as well as ensuring that the policy was politically viable. According to Harris (2005),

> Those who believed Clinton's mental abacus was calculating only the pol-itics of welfare . . . misread him. . . . Though his critics doubted it, the long trajectory of Clinton's involvement with welfare reform—he first began working on the issue in the 1980s—plainly suggested he was drawn to the idea as a matter of genuine principle. In any event, the current system was hard to defend. It had trapped many recipients in cycles of dependency and failure, robbing them of self-esteem and offering no clear path to self-improvement. Yet leaving the poor to their own devices, as he believed many Republicans were content to do, was likewise a moral failure. On purely substantive grounds, the bill the Republican majority had put before him was a close call: Was it better than the status quo? (p. 233).

Clinton believed in the need for people to take more responsibility for their lives and for their children, although he did not want legislation that made life difficult for children in need just because they had irresponsible parents. This position regarding individual responsibility for their actions was at the heart of the idea of the New Democrats in the Democratic Leadership Council (of whom Clinton was the acknowledged leader) and what set them apart from more traditionally liberal Democrats such as those who had developed President Johnson's "War on Poverty" in the 1960s. Indeed, although President Clinton had run on the idea of radically changing welfare, he was definitely not going to accept just any welfare reform package. The president had vetoed two Republican bills because he found them too objectionable, and had worked to mitigate the worst elements of the conservative approach. In the end, for example, he had compromised by including a lifetime limit on welfare receipt, but had wrested from the Republicans progressive provisions for day care, school lunches, health care for children, food stamps, and even a contingency fund to support TANF programs in case of an economic downturn. Clinton worked diligently to restore benefits for immigrants but was unable to get this into the legislation, a point that angered him greatly (Hamilton, 2007).

Another factor impacting Clinton's view of what to do was the quickly approaching election of 1996. While it seemed that Clinton had a comfortable lead over Republican nominee Robert Dole, elections are never won until after the ballots are counted and the Electoral College has voted. Dick Morris had helped Clinton craft a strategy that would weaken the ability of the Republicans to win the White House: the Democrats would work with Republicans in Congress to pass important legislation supported by the public and many conservative legislators in order to keep Dole from using these issues against the president in the election. Welfare reform was one of these issues. Clinton and some of his political advisors believed that this was an issue to resolve, as best they could, to protect their chance of obtaining a second term. Even Dole saw the Clinton/Morris strategy as effective. Dole communicated to the Senate majority leader, Trent Lott, that welfare reform legislation should not be passed because it would make the president look good and take the issue from Dole's arsenal (Lott, 2005).

Clinton was advised by those close to him that this third Republican welfare bill was as good a bill as he would have the chance to sign

(Gillon, 2008; Hamilton, 2007; Harris, 2005; Haskins, 2006; and Lott, 2005). If the bill was vetoed, additional Democratic members of Congress would lose their seats, and the larger Republican majority, empowered by those election results, would come back with a bill that was worse for the Democrats and pass it with a veto-proof majority. Holding out for a better bill would ensure a worse one.

In announcing that he would sign the bill, Clinton declared:

> I made my principles for real welfare reform very clear from the beginning. First and foremost, it should be about moving people from welfare to work. It should impose time limits on welfare. It should give people the child care and the health care they need to move from welfare to work without hurting their children. It should crack down on child-support enforcement, and it should protect our children. . . .
>
> I am deeply disappointed that the Congressional leadership insisted on attaching to this extraordinarily important bill a provision that will hurt legal immigrants in America, people who work hard for their families, pay taxes, serve in our military. This provision has nothing to do with welfare reform; it is simply a budget saving measure, and it is not right (Clinton, 1996).

Clinton's perceptions relating to welfare reform were affected by his history as a governor, and in seeing how the Republican-led changes would affect ordinary Americans and legal immigrants. According to Dick Morris, "As he pondered the fate of immigrants cut off from benefits under the GOP [Republican] bill, he [Clinton] was at this empathetic best, cutting through a policy debate to feel the human pain underneath" (2004, p. 67). This executive branch experience and these feelings of empathy helped determine his preferred course of action, as laid out in his fights with Congress to keep major amounts of funds for child health and child care for all welfare recipients and to allow legal immigrants to keep Medicaid benefits. His opposition to service cuts to legal immigrants was not enough to carry the day in 1996, but he continued working on the topic, and these services were later restored.

Majority Leader Senator Lott Senator Lott had his own reasons for wanting to pass legislation changing the welfare system drastically. After Dick Morris suggested to Lott that President Clinton and he should work together to pass legislation in 1995 and 1996, Lott began to believe that the Republican party would get considerable credit among voters for bipartisanship and working to accomplish significant legislative achievements, including welfare reform. As Lott describes himself:

> I've always had a great enthusiasm for making law—and I believe that that was why my constituents sent me to the Senate in the first place. It seemed to me that if we failed to do these important things, they weren't going to get done—at least any time soon. Of course I have a set of strong philosophical principles. But what good is an unbending purist position if you don't produce results for the people you care about and your country? (Lott, 2005, p. 131).

Lott's perceptions were affected by his strong conservative philosophy and his earlier House of Representatives experiences working with Newt Gingrich and other conservatives in the House. Lott wanted to maintain the Republican majority in the Senate (and House) more than he wanted a Republican president, so he would work across the aisle with Democratic President Clinton, and behind the scenes, to make that happen.

Speaker Gingrich. While Gingrich and Lott had been in the House of Representatives together, Gingrich had a much stronger personality and the desire to do battle with trends and legislation that threatened his view of American civilization. Lott writes: "I could never have done what Newt did to win the majority. I could never have torn down the institution in order to rebuild it. But it worked beautifully for him" (Lott, 2005, p. 128). Gingrich was prepared to use highly controversial tactics to help the Republicans win.

One of his talents was to gather other conservative Congressmen around him, men who were attracted by his passion and intellectual defense of his ideas. Examples included Representatives Dick Armey and Tom DeLay of Texas, and Robert Livingston of Louisiana. Gingrich saw the entire counterculture of the 1960s as the enemy of American civilization, and he was going to be the leader to save it no matter the cost to others. According to Blumenthal (2003), "Gingrich practiced and perfected a politics of annihilation and brought what came to be known as the 'politics of personal destruction' into the modern era" (p. 125). These tactics were used to attack Democratic Speaker of the House Jim Wright, in 1989, on ethics charges, leading to his resignation, and also spread rumors that the next Speaker, Thomas Foley, was gay (Blumenthal, p. 127). Gingrich also had no qualms about demonizing the entire Democratic party. A polling company hired by Gingrich developed a set of words to be used about Democrats at every opportunity—words such as sick, pathetic, liberal, waste, and traitor (Blumenthal, p. 127).

Yet Gingrich also saw that the Republicans needed to offer an alternative. This was the inspiration for the Contract with America. Although there is empirical evidence that it swayed relatively few votes and most of it was never enacted (Blumenthal, 2003, p. 135), it was a new way of approaching campaigning for a party that had not been in the driver's seat for 40 years.

In the end, Gingrich wanted to work out a welfare reform bill that Clinton would sign, just as Lott did. In fact, Gingrich was more powerful in his position as Speaker of the House if Clinton was reelected than if the Republican nominee, Robert Dole, were elected. If a Republican sat in the Oval Office, less attention would be paid to the Speaker of the House than if a Democrat remained in the White House. Thus, in the end, cooperation and compromise of a sort in order to reach an agreement was seen as more valuable than continued intransigence.

What *factors* account for each player's impact on the choice and action?

For each of the three main actors we have examined here, two main factors are important: position and personality. The first is their position in the policy-making hierarchy. It is unlikely that Bill Clinton, Trent Lott, or Newt Gingrich, as ordinary citizens, would have been involved to the extent that they were or that they would have had anywhere near the impact they had. Even if they had been the governor of Arkansas (Clinton), one of two senators from Mississippi (or one out of 100 senators) (Lott) or a representative from Georgia (or one out of 435 representatives), these men would not have had the impact they actually had on the final decision.

Presidential aide and biographer Sidney Blumenthal describes the importance of the top office in the land. "The presidency is the chief engine of progress in American history: its leadership and power are central. No social movement, however broad or righteous, from abolition to labor rights, has seen its aims made into law without presidential power" (2003, p. 12). Still, presidential power is markedly limited: as has been famously noted, "Presidential power is the power to persuade" (Neustadt, 1990, p 11). The president has considerable bargaining power but it must be used vigorously and skillfully. Even in the White House, the president does not always get exactly what he wants, as decisions made by lower-level officials constantly constrain his choices (Allison and Zelikow, 1999).

The positions of Senate majority leader and Speaker of the House are vital to getting any bill passed in their respective chamber. The Speaker's position, for example, had been growing in power before Gingrich came to office, but he planned to make it even more powerful (Hamilton, 2007; Haskins, 2006).

> For a decade, the Speaker's power in the House had steadily been grow-
> ing, as his fiefdom encompassed not only the bills to be heard, via the
> Rules Committee, but the naming of chairmen to all House committees,
> and majority members of those committees. . . . Gingrich now not only
> ended the traditional seniority basis for such appointments but limited
> each chairman's term to six years and cancelled the use of "proxy" votes
> of absent committee members (Hamilton, 2007, p. 406).

The majority leader in the Senate has a position more powerful than that of other senators, of course, but the traditions of the Senate provide each member greater autonomy than representatives have in the House of Representatives. Both the Speaker and the majority leader could lose their position should the membership stage a revolt. Gingrich, for example, had to quell an uprising against his leadership that left him less able to push his agenda (Gillon, 2008). Nonetheless, positional authority, even if constrained, is the most important factor in assessing why Clinton, Lott, and Gingrich had the pivotal impact they had.

In addition, however, each of these players had personal desires to affect this particular decision. One can imagine that Bill Clinton, as the president of the United States, had many competing demands on his time. But he was himself very interested in the topic of welfare policy, having been governor of Arkansas and seeing the way that federal income assistance affected the people of his state, poor and non-poor alike. He had decided to campaign on "ending welfare as we know it" when he ran for president, and had made this one of his signature issues. As noted above, at least one biographer believes this interest was not merely a political calculation, but rather a sincere interest.

Lott describes himself as an ideological person, with strong conservative beliefs. For this reason, he believed people should work rather than be on welfare (Lott, 2005). His views were much in line with the beliefs of the people of the state of Mississippi, and this connection assuredly was no accident. Among other legislation, Lott wanted to pass welfare reform because he believed it was the correct policy prescription.

But Lott was not merely being driven by what he saw as a good policy. He championed the passage of welfare reform despite the desires of Robert Dole, the Republican candidate for president. Dole wanted to kill the bill or keep it so full of objectionable elements that Clinton would veto it. Dole would then use the failure of welfare reform to attack Clinton in the presidential campaign. Lott believed that passing the legislation would help Republicans retain their majority in the Senate by being reelected, and this was a higher priority for him than was having a Republican in the White House. "I heard Dole's concerns. But I had the Senate and House elections to consider. Passing this bill would add political luster to each and every congressman and senator out on the stump. So we passed it, with the votes in both chambers that were veto-proof" (Lott, 2005, pp. 139–140).

Gingrich had an even larger agenda. He wanted to remake the country. In a speech he gave on cable television, he stated: "All of us together—Republicans and Democrats alike—must totally remake the federal government, to change the very way it thinks, the way it does business, the way it treats its citizens" (Hamilton, 2007, p. 434). This plan included as much elimination of welfare to poor citizens as was possible. The Gingrich-crafted Republican Contract with America promised to bring to the floor of the House, within 100 days, the Personal Responsibility Act, which would "discourage illegitimacy and teen pregnancy by prohibiting welfare to minor mothers and denying increased AFDC for additional children while on welfare, cut spending for welfare programs, and enact a tough two-years-and-out provision with work requirements to promote individual responsibility" (Gingrich, 2005, p. 195).

Gingrich knew that more than 60% of Americans agreed with these positions, according to polling data, as well as the other plans put forth in the Contract with America set forth in 1994. Even though Democrats were dismissive of the content, Republicans, after taking over the Senate and the House in the elections of 1994, credited these ideas with their victories (eight new Republican senators and 54 new representatives).

Gingrich and the dozens of other conservatives voted into office had many incentives to try to reform welfare: it was popular with voters; they had made a campaign promise, as strong as President Clinton's, to change the system; and it fit with their laissez-faire economic principles. For Gingrich, personally, making this promise meant getting the job as Speaker of the House, a significant promotion. Now that he was in the position, he did not want to lose it.

What is the "*action channel*," that is, the established process for aggregating competing perceptions, preferences, and stands of players in making decisions and taking action?

The answer to this question is fairly straightforward, at least in theory. In the American governmental system, with two chambers, the House of Representatives and the Senate each pass legislation. If the bills that emerge are not identical, a conference committee is appointed, with members of both the majority and the minority party (naturally, the majority party has more members than the minority party). This committee develops a single bill that is then sent back to the full chamber. If the conference committee has done its job well, then the bill will be passed and sent to the president for signature.

The conference committee bill is difficult enough to create when there are differences between the Senate and the House and it is the same political party that is in the majority in the two chambers. The process becomes even more difficult if one chamber is controlled by the Democrats and the other is controlled by the Republicans. In 1996, however, the Republicans had the majority in both the House and the Senate. This does not necessarily lead to easy decisions, however, as even members of the same party may have different interests, and passing a particular bill may lead to different repercussions for the two bodies. During the conference committee stage, it is also possible for non-members to try to exert influence, and lobbying groups attempt to insert special provisions in the bill. The president and his supporters are also sending information about what he will or will not support, and what provisions would be so anathema that he would veto it. If both chambers of Congress have fewer votes in favor of the bill than the two-thirds majority (of those voting) required to override a presidential veto, the threat of a veto is very strong, although not always something to be scared of. With welfare reform, for example, Republican candidate Dole wanted President Clinton to be forced to veto a welfare reform bill for the third time.

Once both chambers have gone through this process, the bill is sent to the White House for signature. At that point, the president may:

- sign the bill within ten days (and thus it becomes law);
- veto the bill directly (at which time the bill is dead, unless both the Senate and the House of Representatives override the veto with a two-thirds majority vote in its favor); or
- take no action on the bill, which has two possible outcomes: if Congress remains in session for the ten days after sending the bill to the president, the bill becomes law without his signature; if Congress adjourns during this ten-day period, then the bill is killed (this is termed an *indirect*, or *pocket*, veto).

In order to reach this decision, each president has had his own process. Clinton assembled his own team of advisors, as described earlier, heard the arguments on both sides, and in the end said, "That's it. I'll sign it" (Haskins, 2006, p. 329).

Of course, this is just the official "how a bill becomes law" civics class sort of institutional explanation. Detailed accounts of the passage of any controversial legislation often have long, blow-by-blow descriptions of key negotiation sessions between the most important players and how peripheral actors stepped in at the last moment to possibly threaten the successful conclusion of the process. Ron Haskins (2006), a Republican staffer working closely on the welfare reform bills, has written such an account. It makes for fascinating reading and brings to mind the adage that one should not know too much about how sausage and legislation are made. At 428 pages in length, it is truly the sort of book that relatively few people will read cover-to-cover, yet it explains the twists and turns of the legislative process exquisitely.

CONCLUSION

This chapter has examined a second approach to understanding the enactment of social policy: the power and politics model. By examining the positions, politics, and relative power of each of the main participants, we have a more nuanced view of the policy-making process. We can see the importance of the rules of the policy creation game, such as the way that leaders of the Senate and the House are chosen and the powers they wield; the structure of government with federalism, separation of powers, and checks and balances. We can also see how important the person who sits in the position is. An incumbent without the ability or will to actually lead will not be able to move the legislation along. Finally, we can also see glimmers of how useful possible underlying political views (such as pluralism and elitism) are in helping us understand a large number of details.

By using this approach, compared to the historical, we have a better view of what happened and why it happened. Policy is more than just random actions leading to unpredictable outcomes. Who is involved, under what rules, and when, are important issues for all policy analysts.

4

Using the "Rational Actor" Approach

This chapter is about analyzing policy formation from the "*rational actor*" perspective. Perhaps more than any other policy approach, it is both commonly used and commonly attacked (see Ward, 2003, for a longer overview of the debate). Variations of the comprehensive rational approach, such as "bounded rationality" (Simon, 1982; 1985) have been developed to address common criticisms. A rational approach is sometimes seen as the "gold standard" in policy and other discussions and is often seen as the antithesis of the political model described in the previous chapter. In this chapter, we will examine what is meant by the *rational* and *bounded rational actor* models, how to use them, and what their strengths and weaknesses are, and then apply the rational model to the same case that we have been using, the creation of the Temporary Assistance for Needy Families program, as passed in the Personal Responsibility and Work Opportunities Reconciliation Act. We also examine the differences between users of the rational model and its variants in *creating* policy, on one hand, and *analyzing* policy after the fact, on the other.

DESCRIPTION OF THE RATIONAL APPROACH

Traditional economic and rational policy analysis is perhaps epitomized by Bardach (2005), Gupta (2001), or Patton and Sawicki (1993). The focus for anyone using a rational approach is on construct-ing goals and seeking the most efficient means of achieving those goals. While referring to nuclear deterrence, Thomas Schelling's description of the foundation of the rational actor approach still holds for other policy types as well. The key element is "the assumption of rational behavior—not just of intelligent behavior, but of behavior motivated by a conscious calculation of advantages, a calculation that in turn is based on an explicit and internally consistent value system" (Schelling, cited in Allison and Zelikow, 1999, p. 15). Jones, Boushey, and Workman (2006) argue that rational choice models have two characteristics in common, regardless of their other differences. The first characteristic assumption is that "decision-makers hold stable *ranked* and *ordered* preferences for outcomes" (emphasis in original, p. 51). Second, decision makers have sufficient information to link behavioral choices to outcomes and can thus optimize their decisions. March (1994) also indicates that in the comprehensive rational actor model, decision makers theoretically have no constraints on time or other resources. To be rational actors, then, means that decision-makers try to efficiently maximize gains and minimize losses as they consis-tently support their primary values, having all the time and resources desired.

In an interesting way, the rational approach is based on something entirely non-rational. Rational behavior, in this sense, is about realizing values, or promoting an ideology. Rational behavior is thus in service of something larger than the behavior. Rationality (a decision-making process) is but a tool to achieve something that is not, and cannot be, successfully defended by logic alone. Whether one values a pro-life or a pro-choice position on abortion; whether one supports providing extensive or limited government assistance to the poor, or whether one promotes or is against capital punishment—these beliefs are primarily a question of values and ideology, and the purely rational policy actor cannot provide an overwhelmingly powerful argument to someone who has a contrary value or who accepts a differ-ent ideology.

The typical rational approach can be described as a list of steps, such as:

- *Define the problem* (that is, in what ways does the current situation affect the actor's values?).
- *Determine evaluation criteria* (which are based on the actor's goals and objectives).
- *Identify alternative policies.*
- *Evaluate the alternative policies* to decide which will attain the most or lose the least ground relating to one's desired values.
- *Select the preferred policy* (the one which attains the most or loses the least).
- *Implement the preferred policy* (Patton and Sawicki, 1993, p. 2).

Comprehensive rationality assumes "the actor has reviewed *all* alternatives, and accurately assesses *all* consequences in make the value-maximizing choice. In contrast, *bounded rationality* recognizes inescapable limitations of knowledge and computational ability of the agent" (Allison and Zelikow, 1999, p. 20; emphases in original). Bounded rationality admits that decision-makers commit errors in judgment based on limited knowledge, mistakes in thinking, and not having enough time or funding to collect all the information that might be helpful. Making such errors does not mean that the decision-makers are "irrational"—but it indicates that a comprehensive approach to rationality is probably impossible.

Instead of searching for the "best" option possible, the bounded rationality model describes what decision-makers do as *satisficing*— looking for solutions that are "good enough" to meet the minimum needs of the decision-making situation (March and Simon, 1958). "Satisficing" requires limited information about the problem, the options to solve the problem, and the probable effects of each solution considered. While this may seem a far cry from the notion of comprehensive rationality described earlier, they agree in the underlying notion that people choose a solution that meets their needs as best they can, based on the information that they have in front of them, in order to achieve as much of their cherished values as possible.

INFORMATION NEEDED TO USE THE RATIONAL APPROACH

Herbert Simon, one of the pioneers in exploring differences between comprehensive and bounded rationality, has answered the question of what information is needed quite neatly. According to Allison and Zelikow (1999):

> Simon underlines the difference between comprehensive and bounded rationality as follows. To deduce the comprehensive rational choice in a given situation, "we need to know only the choosing organism's goals and the objective characteristics of the situation. We need to know absolutely nothing else about the organism." In contrast, to deduce the boundedly rational choice in the same situation, "we must know the choosing organism's goals, the information and conceptualization it has of the situation, and its abilities to draw inferences from the information it possesses" (p. 20).

Let us take a simple, non-policy example. A mother wants to buy her 17-year-old son a car so he can drive himself to school, his job, and other places. Her major priority is for him to have a very safe vehicle. The objective characteristics of the situation are that she only has $5,000 to spend, and she lives in a bedroom community to a large city, but that the son will be expected to drive only around the suburban area. Ultimately, the car the mother buys is a blue five-year-old Honda Civic with 117,000 miles on it. If we ask ourselves, using the comprehensive rational actor approach, "Why this car?" we could answer that, of all the cars available in the mother's price rang in the entire metropolitan area, this seemed the safest. Even though it has comparatively many miles on it, the Honda brand is known for lasting a long time, and the Civic has a very good safety record.

Taking the boundedly rational approach, we need to provide more details about the decision to opt for this vehicle. For example, additional information relating to the car's purchase is that the mother wanted to spend no more than a weekend looking, did not have access to the internet at home, and had asked a family friend who was a former Honda car mechanic to help in the decision-making process. The mother herself had driven a Honda since she began driving at age 16, and had been in a collision (no fault of hers) in a Civic but had walked away unhurt from that wreck. She also admitted that she knew little about other brands of cars. With this information, we might argue that the purchase came about as the result of a much-less-than-comprehensive look at all the cars for sale. The mother looked only at nearby sources for used cars, favoring a Honda dealership with used vehicles from the start. From her own experiences, the mother believed that Civics are safe vehicles and are well able to protect the occupants of the car if an accident should occur. Being rather short of time, her basic choice was between a "taffeta white" and a "dyno blue pearl" Honda Civic, both of which the family friend inspected for a brief time and pronounced "clean." The son wanted a "San Marino red" Accord with leather seats, but none were available in the mother's price range, so he opted for the blue Civic to match one of his high school's colors.

The second explanation presents what most people would believe is a "truer" account of the outcome: the mother purchased a blue Honda Civic for her son. Understanding the limits of rationality, including the need to decide using no more than a certain amount of resources, within a certain amount of time, amongst a limited number of options, and with the advice of a certain group of people, provides a more realistic description of choices for social policy-making, as well.

Rational analysis can take place at several different points in the policy cycle (Gupta, 2001). Starting with the agenda-setting stage, the policy cycle continues to policy formulation, policy adoption, policy implementation, policy evaluation, and may end with policy termination. Policy, instead of ending, may also change, leading to additional agenda-setting, and so on. For the purposes of this chapter, we focus on the policy formulation stage, as we are seeking to explain policy creation.

Within the policy formulation stage, one of the first steps is to understand the causes of the behaviors we want to change. Gupta refers to developing a "behavioral model" (2001, p. 57), which makes assumptions about human nature. In the case of welfare policy, we would try to include in our behavioral model implicit or explicit explanations of welfare recipients' behaviors. We want answers to questions such as, "Why do people apply for welfare, in the first place?" "Why do people stay on welfare?" and "How can we get people on welfare off the rolls?" Only by trying to understand why people act the way they do can we hope to change those behaviors.

Schiller (2007) describes three basic mental models for understanding why people are poor. The first model that some people believe is that the poor are basically to blame for their own poverty because they have some sort of individual flaw that puts them below the poverty line and keeps them there. It may be that the poor are "lazy" and do not want to work; or they may be under-educated for the jobs available and cannot find employment. Using a second behavioral model, other people believe that the poor are really more victims of injustices than architects of their own poverty. Centuries of slavery and economic exploitation, they explain, condemn millions of minority adults, youth, and children to continued existences on the margins of society. Finally, a third model that some people accept is that programs have created a set of dependent individuals who rely on government or nonprofit assistance rather than taking responsibility to provide for themselves and their families.

These models influence what decision-makers believe should be done to solve the problem. If the poor are lazy and likely to lean on government programs, the best way to keep them from being dependent is to remove the crutch of government support. Time limits for receipt, for example, will provide an incentive to get some job experience or additional education and job-skills training. On the other hand, if one believes that the poor are victims of an uncaring capitalistic society, the policy alternatives that make more sense are to work in the political realm to strengthen the earned income tax credit or to develop new programs that will improve life chances for the poor. One may use a needs assessment to determine what the current situation is and what gaps should be overcome. If one believes that government and nonprofit programs, themselves, cause dependency, then the policy solution is to eliminate those programs.

To summarize this section, in order to understand policy creation using the rational and bounded rationality approaches, we need to be able to answer the following questions:

- What are the goals (desired end states) of the key actors?
- What are the objective characteristics of the situation?
- How closely did the key actors come to getting what they wanted?

ADVANTAGES OF THE RATIONAL APPROACH

Jones et al. (2006) believe that the rational actor model has three important benefits. First, the rational approach is parsimonious. It needs very little in the way of information, yet it can usefully be applied to a wide range of topics. By determining the range of probable payoffs to the decision-makers, and assuming that they will make the choice that provides them the largest payoff, a great deal of behavior can be predicted and understood. Secondly, the rational actor model can be generalized across actors and time. Decisions are thought to be made to increase the person's "happiness" in the past, now, and in the future. It is not necessary to infer other motivations. Finally, rational actor models are testable mathematically; this encourages careful model creation and development so that variables in the models will have empirical support.

The key advantage of the rational approach is that "it works." That is, given a limited amount of information, and a limited amount of time in which to gather additional information, the assumption of rationality is a useful shortcut that accurately provides a guide to an actor's decisions. "By exploring the strategic behavior of self-interested individuals, rational choice theorists have produced a rich and theoretically unified body of research in a discipline once marked by methodological eclecticism" (Jones et al., 2006, p. 52). Most people, when asked, put their behavior into a logical framework, explaining how decisions they made were in their best interest, helped them achieve their goals, and were in line with their previous behavior. This understanding of their behavior may all be created after the fact, however, and other factors may actually have been much more important at the time. Once an understanding of the bounds of rationality is included in the description of the decisions, the rational approach seems even more likely to produce a story that rings true. Thus, the assumptions behind the rational actor model help us understand past, current, and future decisions on the individual level.

Rational analysis (the primary set of tools used by rational actors) is used to understand policy problems and to fashion solutions that have an increased probability of solving those problems. While the answers derived in this way may or may not be convincing on their own, they help set the boundaries of reasonable proposals. The building of a bridge may provide a useful analogy. The bridge's architect may have strong beliefs about the aesthetics of the design, and that certain elements should look a certain way, but if the engineer cannot incorporate the correct load-stress factors and other empirically derived elements of bridge-building into the artistic vision, the bridge will not stay up for long. Similarly, even though policy decision-makers may have political goals in mind more than substantive policy goals, if politicians ignore policy analysts altogether, the policy may lead to a disaster, and the blame may come back to haunt the officials who voted for it. Thus, an understanding of rational policy analysis tools is important in understanding how policy is constructed.

Rational Policy Analysis Tools

The policy process often begins with analysis of a current situation; once solutions are identified, analysis forecasts what will happen if they are implemented. A few of the analytical techniques that are used to do this (moving from least to most sophisticated) are: educated guessing, interviewing of experts, using existing official descriptive data, and conducting more advanced statistical analyses. The following section describes these methods and notes potential problems with each technique.

Educated Guessing

While it may seem inappropriate to call "guessing" an analytical technique, there are some reasons to turn to it as a starting point. First, educated guessing may be used to quickly rule out some interpretations of the situation or some possible effects of a potential solution. For example, an educated guess could tell us that the problem of welfare dependency in urban areas is not the same as in rural areas, nor are the solutions likely to be the same. Second, educated guessing can be useful when trying to understand big-picture questions of this sort: "Is this a big problem? About how large is it? Why is it happening? Is there anything we can do about it?"

The value of educated guessing is based largely on the amount of education that is involved relative to the amount of guessing. Patton and Sawicki (1993) list eight different approaches to educated guessing that are really different forms of extrapolating from known information. Assuming that the numbers used to extrapolate from are accurate and the approaches to extrapolation are reasonable, the results can be quite useful. Examples of the techniques noted by Patton and Sawicki are to apply relatively unvarying rates to a population to derive an estimated number of people affected by a situation; to create a reasonable estimate based on the results of several independent estimates (triangulation); or to apply a rate from a similar phenomenon (see Patton and Sawicki for more information). For example, given the costs and results of a job-training program in one city, an analyst might be able to estimate (make an educated guess) what the costs of achieving similar results in a different locale would be, taking into account how similar or different the two locations are.

In the analysis leading up to the welfare reform bill in 1996, a great deal of information had been collected on the number of people on welfare, the rates of AFDC receipt, the lengths of welfare stints, as well as the effects of many "welfare experiments" that had been tried at the state level. Still, the debates within Congress and the White House at times used estimates that could be called "educated guessing" but with an ideological bias of considerable proportions. One particularly contentious issue that led to wide differences in estimates was the probable results of the TANF legislation on poverty rates and the impacts on individuals who used up their welfare eligibility. As noted on the ten-year anniversary of the legislation, estimates of the problems that TANF would cause were inaccurate on many accounts:

> At the time, most American liberals predicted disaster. As Katha Pollitt wrote in *The New Republic*, "wages will go down, families will fracture, millions of children will be made more miserable than ever." One frequently cited study predicted that more than a million children would be thrown into poverty. Welfare advocates painted vivid pictures of families sleeping on sidewalks, widespread starvation, and worse. The *New York Times* opined, "the effect on our cities will be devastating." Senator Frank Lautenberg, a Democrat of New Jersey, predicted "hungry and homeless children" would be walking our streets "begging for money, begging for food, even . . . engaging in prostitution." *The Nation* prophesied that "people will die, businesses will close, infant mortality will soar" (Tanner, 2006).

Educated guessing is not only acceptable when no firm data are available, it is necessary. Data are sometimes not collected for political reasons, as the information would indicate that a problem exists that some people do not want to acknowledge. Data may also not be available for a specific jurisdiction or area, such as at the county, city, or neighborhood level. In addition, when looking to the future, no one knows for certain what will happen. It is in situations such as these that educated guessing is not only an appropriate technique, but possibly the only available technique. Caution is still advised when making or using educated guesses due to the inherent problems of the method.

Interviewing of Experts

Analysts who need to quickly come up with recommendations often turn to identified experts as a way to shorten their learning curve and come up with defensible estimates of the situation and probable effects of specific policy options. Experts, of course, have varying levels of expertise and, possibly more worrying, varying levels of objectivity. Experts may shade their opinions, knowingly or not, depending on the results they want to see from the policy in question. Analysts relying on others for their information need to understand the limits of the people they interview. Purposely choosing informants of different ideological or political views can assist one in finding a middle ground that may be more accurate. The technique of triangulation is an especially important one to use in this situation.

Official Descriptive Data

Governmental and other organizations frequently collect and publish the results of data collection efforts that strive to be objective. Still, certain issues of definition and data collection should be understood. The Census Bureau, for example, creates estimates of the size of the population between the decennial censuses. These numbers are used in many ways, such as to determine funding for some government programs. The Census Bureau also publishes information on poverty, which is important in understanding the size of the problem and its trends. The Census Bureau clearly identifies the methodology used and the statistical limits of their numbers. Here is the statement they make on one publication: "For information on sampling and estimation methods, confidentiality protection, and sampling and nonsampling errors, please see the '2009 ACS Accuracy of the Data' document located at www.census.gov/acs/ www/Downloads/data_documentation/Accuracy/ACS_Accuracy_of_ Data_2009.pdf" (United States Census Bureau, 2010, p. 4).

Despite this transparency, there is considerable debate over the definition of poverty. There are actually several definitions of *poverty* published by the Census Bureau, using different procedures, all of which have specific assumptions built into them. The definition that has been used since the early 1960s, for example, takes the cost of the Thrifty Food Plan promulgated by the Department of Agriculture and multiplies it by three. This formula was developed because, at the time of its creation, the average family in the United States spent one-third of their income on food. This proportion has changed in the last 50 years, but the formula has not. Other means of calculating poverty have been created and are reported, but this particular definition lives on in order to maintain continuity and comparability over time (DiNitto, 2007).

Collection procedures are another source of error in the data. Information related to crimes, for example, is reported to the Federal Bureau of Investigation and is reported to the public as Uniform Crime Statistics. Critics of these numbers point to the lack of uniformity in the data caused by different procedures used in the reporting jurisdictions across the country. Poverty numbers, for another example, are based primarily on self-reports of individuals who have an incentive to under-report their income. This may lead to distortions of the final figures used in policy decisions.

Once obtained, official data may be manipulated using basic statistical procedures to produce means, averages, rates, and so on, that may be useful. These basic numbers are often graphed or otherwise depicted pictorially in order to emphasize their meaning. Even here, the analyst must be careful in how the numbers are displayed, or else the picture painted can be misleading.

The important point for users of official descriptive data such as these that are seemingly objective is that one must understand the nuances of the definition and collection methods used to develop them. This is even truer of the statistics published by other sources that have a more biased agenda (Best, 2001).

An egregious example of the misuse of simple data analysis is Charles Murray's 1984 book, *Losing Ground*, which was used to justify cuts in welfare spending during the Reagan administration. Murray argues that it is welfare itself that causes its recipients to become dependent. One critical review of his book states: "He says an intellectual elite shifted the blame for poverty, crime and low achievement to 'the system' destroying individual responsibility. But his argument is not supported by evidence. Data are bent to fit foregone conclusions" (Dolbeare and Lidman, 1985, p. 587).

More Advanced Statistical Analyses

Everything that is true of the creation and use of simple descriptive data is also true of advanced statistical analyses. Multivariate data analysis and modeling are seen as a way to create a better understanding of a phenomenon, including forecasting the effects of proposed policies (Gupta, 2001; Patton and Sawicki, 1993), yet (usually) these same models use data developed by others and incorporate assumptions that are not always clearly specified. Advanced modeling can cover inadequate thinking about the underlying policy issues at stake (Banks, 1992). The dangers of modeling are well stated by Banks (1992, p. v):

> Potentially undesirable consequences of these difficulties include using models to rationalize institutional prejudices, poor models driving out careful thinking, and tending to emphasize those aspects of a problem that can best be simulated. The result can often be that computer models provide an illusion of analytic certainty for problems that are not that well understood or, in the worst cases, provide scientific costume for points of view that are self-serving.

The principle of *caveat emptor* applies very strongly—the policy analyst who "buys" someone else's analysis must be extremely careful in deciding how much to rely on it.

Analysts who develop their own models, based on their own carefully collected data, have greater understanding of the pluses and minuses of the information that they derive. Decision makers who truly do not have a biased agenda can receive insight from advanced statistical results. Such methods allow for clearer understanding of the causes of problems and the impacts of possible solutions (Gupta, 2001).

CRITIQUES OF THE RATIONAL APPROACH

Hudson and Low (2009) discuss two problems with the rational actor theory (whether comprehensive or bounded): the collective action problem and altruism. Both stem from the premise that rational actors are motivated strictly by their own self-interest. An example of the "collective-action problem" (discussed at length by Olson, 1965) is when people join an organization (at some cost) with no expectation of receiving a benefit commensurate with the cost. Organizations frequently attempt to overcome the perception that the cost of joining is higher than the benefits by promoting the range of member benefits, tangible and intangible. Tangible benefits include magazine or journal subscriptions, newsletters, discounts on products, and educational or social opportunities. Intangible benefits are things such as opportunities for involvement, networking, and helping to overcome social problems. Another type of collective-action problem occurs when a person decides not to join a benefit-providing organization when the benefit can be enjoyed without joining. (This is also known as the "free rider" problem.) There is no "rational" reason to take on the cost in either case, yet such behavior is common.

An example may help clarify these ideas. Consider social workers deciding whether or not to join the National Association of Social Workers. There is a definite cost involved. Benefits are also provided. Tangible benefits include a subscription to the journal *Social Work*, email alerts, opportunities for free continuing-education credits, and so on. Intangible benefits include networking at meetings, the opportunity to attend an annual conference, and the good things that come from the efforts of NASW lobbyists. Rational people take a look at the value of the benefits that come with the membership, discounting some of them because they are not of importance to them (perhaps these people do not enjoy networking events, for instance, so this is not considered of much or any value), and discounting other benefits, such as lobbying, because the benefit helps all social workers whether they join NASW or not. In the end, for the rational actor, the question comes down to answering whether the benefits outweigh the costs to the individual making the decision. Still, some people join because they feel it is "the right thing to do," and NASW overcomes the collective-action problem of getting social workers to join, even though there is no compelling rational reason to do so.

Altruism, the feeling and behavior of putting the needs of others ahead of one's own, is also a problem for rational actor analysts because it is antithetical to a selfish rational look at costs and gains. People donate blood and money with no expectation of receiving something in return; people allow women who are pregnant to sit on a bus while they stand. While an argument can be made that performing these acts makes people feel good about themselves, so it is a rational, and self-interested behavior, this argument is tautological—there is no way to disprove it.

Charles Lindblom (1955) presents a different challenge to rational decision making and policy planning. In his estimation, policy making and implementation are simply too complex for us to be able to understand all the causes of problems, potential solutions, and the actual effects of a policy once enacted and implemented. In other words, the world is too complex for rationality to be successful. He thus advocates an incremental process, which he terms "muddling through," to make small changes in policy, note the successes and problems with the new policy, and then make additional incremental change. Done in this way, policy is likely to be more successful and more adaptable to the changing situations in peoples' lives.

APPLICATION OF THE RATIONAL APPROACH

In this section, we will examine the actions of the three key players, President Bill Clinton, Speaker Newt Gingrich, and Senate Majority Leader Trent Lott, as in previous chapters.

What are the goals (desired end states) of the key actors?

We are fortunate in that all of the key players have a record of saying what they were trying to achieve; that is, what their explicit goals were. In this section, we will look at both policy goals and political goals. *Policy goals* are the changes in laws and regulations that are desired; *political goals* are the changes or desired states of running for and gaining office, either for oneself or one's allies.

Bill Clinton

Policy goals
As a candidate, Bill Clinton had promised to "end welfare as we know it." Once in office, he appointed respected academics and others with broad and deep knowledge of welfare issues to develop legislative language.

Mary Jo Bane and David Ellwood were two such Harvard-based appointees. Their proposal had the following goals:

- *Make work pay.* Low-income workers need a living wage, health care, and child care to make working make sense instead of welfare.
- *Two-year limits.* Transform the welfare system from a "handout" to a "hand-up," with clear requirements to work after two years of training or education.
- *Child-support enforcement.* Require absent parents to pay, whether or not they were married.
- *Fight teen pregnancy.* The plan offered grants to high-risk schools that proposed innovative initiatives to lower rates of teen pregnancy and also supported a national clearinghouse and a few intensive demonstration projects. (Zukerman, 2000, p. 589–590)

This legislation was not actively promoted in the first years of the Clinton administration because of the high costs associated with such policies. Because Clinton wanted to also cut the budget deficit (inherited from Republican presidents Ronald Reagan and George H. W. Bush), he decided that welfare reform would take a back seat to deficit reduction and health care reform (Hamilton, 2007; Zukerman, 2000). Clinton's welfare reform proposal, when introduced in 1994, was also a victim of his low standing in the polls, due partially to the failure of health care reform, as well as difficulties in foreign affairs (Zukerman, 2000).

Even though Congress was controlled by Democrats prior to 1994, many of the leaders were more liberal than Clinton, and they did not support his welfare reform proposal. Daniel Patrick Moynihan, for example, one of the most prominent senators with real expertise on poverty issues, accused Clinton of cynically using welfare reform only for election purposes and was quoted as saying that passing the Republican welfare reform bill would be "the most brutal act of social policy since Reconstruction" (Harris, 2005, p. 234).

Political goals
The president had a goal of being reelected. Dick Morris, the pollster who also worked with Senator Trent Lott, counseled President Clinton

to sign the bill and fix the parts he did not like later, after he was reelected. Peter Edelman, an assistant secretary of Health and Human Services (and the husband of Marion Wright Edelman, director of the Children's Defense Fund) resigned in protest over the signing of the bill. He believed that Clinton accepted the bill "to make absolutely sure of re-election" (Hamilton, 2007, p. 626).

Newt Gingrich

Policy goals

The legislative goals of the Speaker of the House are laid out in the Contract with America signed on Tuesday, September 27, 1994, by 376 Republican officeholders or candidates for office. The Contract states that the Republican-controlled Congress would bring forth specific pieces of legislation to vote on within 100 days of Congress's coming into session. Point 3, relating to what would be called The Personal Responsibility Act, states that the bill would:

> Discourage illegitimacy and teen pregnancy by prohibiting welfare to minor mothers and denying increased AFDC for additional children while on welfare, cut spending for welfare programs, and enact a tough two-years-and-out provision with work requirements to promote individual responsibility (U.S. House of Representatives, 1994a).

The bill that was introduced by the House leadership after the Republicans won control of both the House and Senate in the 1994 congressional elections is summarized by the House of Representatives in this way:

> The Personal Responsibility Act overhauls the American welfare system to reduce government dependency, attack illegitimacy, require welfare recipients to enter work programs and cap total welfare spending. The bill's main thrust is to give states greater control over the benefits programs, work programs, and Aid to Families with Dependent Children (AFDC) payments and requirements (U.S. House of Representatives, 1994b).

Provisions are described as (1) reducing illegitimacy, (2) requiring work, (3) capping the growth of welfare spending, and (4) [increasing] state flexibility. Two other provisions included preventing discrimination in terms of race, color, or national origin for adoptive parents and requiring welfare recipients who are addicted to drugs to receive treatment and participate in random drug-testing to continue to receive benefits. A final section of the highlights indicates that expected cost savings for the bill were $40 billion, including $22 billion saved from the denial of welfare to non-citizens (U.S. House of Representatives, 1994b).

Political goals

The political goals that Gingrich sought to achieve in 1996 were less to help the Republican candidate for president, former Senate Majority Leader Robert Dole, than they were to embarrass President Clinton and assist the Republicans in their bid to retain control of Congress (Haskins, 2006). If Clinton did not sign a "reasonable" welfare reform bill, he would be attacked as not having fulfilled his campaign promise. If he did, then Republicans could claim credit for being able legislators, thus enhancing their election year standing. One of the key aspects of making a welfare reform bill "reasonable" was to keep it fairly well focused on requiring work in exchange for welfare receipt. To do this required jettisoning a provision that would decrease Medicaid (the health care program for the poor) funding. Fearing that Clinton could portray the Republicans as attacking poor children, and wanting a relatively reasonable bill, the Republicans decided to eliminate the cuts to Medicaid from the welfare reform bill. As described by Haskins (2006), "the struggle to extract the welfare reform rabbit from the Medicaid briar patch was the key to Republicans making progress on their reform agenda and to maintaining their congressional majorities" (p. 305).

Trent Lott

Policy goals

Lott's Republican vision of welfare reform was intended to overcome the myriad problems of the AFDC program. These issues included long-term and intergenerational dependency on welfare, breakdown of the African American family, encouragement of drug use, and fraud and abuse of federal funds (Lott, 2005). The key provisions that were sent forward for negotiation with President Clinton were work in exchange for welfare, time limits, ending welfare's status as an entitlement, creating a welfare block grant to give to states to administer, and converting welfare centers into specialized employment offices (Lott, 2005).

Political goals

The Senate majority leader shared the political goal of helping Republican members of Congress be reelected and to elect additional Republican members. Welfare reform was but one aspect of this overall goal. Lott (2005) wanted to show the electorate that Republicans were the "party of substance and legislative action" (p. 134), which would put them in "an enviable space to occupy as we went into the 1996 elections" (p. 134). Previous to the welfare reform efforts of 1996, the Senate passed legislation that addressed health care portability, concerns over clean drinking water, and some environmental issues. Lott then wanted to move forward with welfare reform and was determined to achieve a breakthrough to overcome the problems in the two earlier bills that Clinton had vetoed.

What are the objective characteristics of the situation?

In order to understand the actions of rational actors, it is vital to understand the situation as it is. It is tempting to say that we must understand the situation as the actors view it (as a constructivist analyst would) but the rational actor model assumes that there is a high degree of overlap between what people believe the situation is and what it actually is. Actors working outside of the objective characteristics of the situation generally have limited success in achieving their goals. So the model seeks to describe the situation in terms of options, benefits, and costs, as well as the risks involved and the actors' willingness to take those risks.

The full rational actor model includes not only objectives but also calculations about the situation in which the actor finds himself. This context presents threats and opportunities that the agent packages as options with pros and cons. The actor chooses the alternative that best advances his interests. Thus in explaining what an actor did, or in making bets about what he is likely to do, an analyst must consider, not only the actor's objectives, but also the options he identifies, the costs and benefits he estimates will follow from each option, and his readiness or reluctance to take risks (Allison and Zelikow, 1999, p. 49).

Here are some of the facts that seem clear as we examine the welfare reform situation:

- Clinton campaigned for president on the issue of welfare reform and had been actively involved with changing AFDC since his days as governor of Arkansas.
- Gingrich's Contract with America put great emphasis on changing welfare programs, as discussed earlier in this chapter.
- The 1996 elections were coming soon. The president wanted to be reelected.
- Bob Dole, the Republican candidate, was behind in the polls and was not going to bring along many votes for members of Congress. It was prudent, therefore, for the leaders of the Senate and the House of Representatives to look out for their own interests rather than attempting to help the Republican nominee for president, if the two things could not be combined. Passing welfare reform legislation was integral to Senator Lott's and Speaker Gingrich's plans for maintaining a Republican majority in Congress, even if it also helped the Democratic president be reelected.
- According to public opinion polls, the American public was in favor of reducing the number of people on welfare and the cost of benefits.
- When it came to the decision of whether President Clinton should sign the bill, opinion among his advisors was divided. But the bill had enough Republican votes to pass, with enough support from Democrats in Congress that the legislation was probably veto-proof.
- The research that might refute the aims of the welfare reform bill was not strong, although advocates against the measure argued that millions of children would become poor and their families be cast adrift in American society (Zukerman, 2000).
- The research being used to support the passage of the bill was not particularly strong either, but it was probably more accurate in terms of the problems of AFDC than the benefits of the proposed law (Haskins, 2006; Zukerman, 2000).

Table 4.1 Benefits and Costs of Cooperating to Get the Bill Passed for Each
Major Actor

Player	Benefits of Cooperating to Get Bill Passed	Costs of Cooperating to Get Bill Passed
Clinton	Achieve most policy goals of welfare reform (policy). Increase chances of own reelection (political).	Enact certain policies in the bill that are very distasteful (policy). Alienate left wing of Democratic party (political). Assist Republicans in Congress to achieve important policy change thus helping them get reelected (political).
Lott	Achieve many policy goals of welfare reform (policy). Increase odds of continuing Republican control of Congress (political).	Assist Clinton in being reelected (political). Possibly alienate the more conservative wing of Republican party in Congress (political).
Gingrich	Achieve many policy goals of welfare reform (policy). Increase odds of continuing Republican control of Congress (political).	Assist Clinton in being reelected (political). Possibly alienate the more conservative wing of Republican party in Congress (political).

We show the basic listing of the benefits and costs of passing the bill for each of the actors in Table 4.1, noting whether they relate to policy or politics.

With these as the probable payoffs, it appears that the most rational action for each of these three players was to work hard to pass a "reasonable" bill that was signed by the president. The second outcome, to not get a bill passed, assisted the Republican presidential candidate, which would have been a clearly negative result for Clinton, but not necessarily a large positive for Lott and Gingrich. A Republican president would naturally take the spotlight off of both Lott and Gingrich. Gingrich, it was said, had presidential aspirations of his own, possibly as early as the election of 2000. If Dole became president in 1996, he could potentially run for reelection in 2000, thus forcing Gingrich to wait four more years, and having to battle a sitting Vice-President for the nomination. In short, there is very little in the way of negatives to passing a bill, but possible problems if the bill were vetoed. Of course, hindsight is 20/20, and at the time the issues regarding welfare reform had to be seen by many Democrats as part of a larger war against the radical nature of the Republican Party plans to dismantle many social service programs. These Democrats wanted to draw a line in the sand and stymie the conservative agenda, at least in the short run.

How close did the key actors come to getting what they wanted?

In the political realm, every one of the three key players' election-related hopes came true. President Clinton was reelected, as was Speaker Gingrich (Senator Lott was not up for reelection in 1996, having been reelected to a six-year term in 1994). The House remained controlled by Republicans, as did the Senate. Thus, using a rational actor model of analysis related to the key actors' *political goals*, we would say that President Clinton, Speaker Gingrich, and Senator Lott were highly successful.

The key actors were also able to get much of what they each wanted in terms of their *policy goals* incorporated into the law that was passed and signed, which indicates that they had considerably overlapping goals. The Personal Responsibility and Work Opportunity Act was designed to eliminate dependency on welfare, encourage work, discourage out-of-wedlock births, and save money. Compromises occurred so that a bill could be passed. The president agreed to a time limit on welfare aid (which the Republicans wanted as a way to decrease dependency and save money), but "leveraged that to obtain broad social provisions—day care, a contingency fund in case of recession, school lunches, health care for children and food stamps" (Blumenthal, 2003, p. 145). As aide Bruce Reed argued to Clinton in July of 1996, "We have already won the battle on virtually every issue that is central to moving people from welfare to work" (Gillon, 2008, p. 178). Senate Majority Leader Lott seemed to feel the Republicans compromised more than their share to reach agreement. For example, funds for child health care and vouchers for child care had considerable monies reinstated compared to earlier versions of the legislation (Lott, 2005). He complained to Dick Morris, the go-between for him and Clinton, when Morris indicated that Clinton wanted further changes made to the bill:

. . .the president's moving the goalposts. You said he wanted school lunches fixed, and we did that. Then you said he wanted day care. Then he

wanted a contingency fund, then the separating out of Medicaid. Now .
you come back with a whole new set of demands. We have caved in on
almost everything, and each time you come back with more, more, more
(Lott, 2005, p. 138).

Despite the areas of compromise and agreement, other issues were not
resolved to everyone's satisfaction. The Republicans rebuffed almost all
efforts to allow immigrants any federal welfare coverage (Medicaid to legal
immigrants was kept). Lott had promised Clinton that this could be made
more to Clinton's liking. When it was not changed, Clinton was livid. "'This
is not about welfare,' he shouted to an aide after hanging up the phone. 'This
is about screwing immigrants and screwing me'" (Gillon, 2008, p. 178).

While President Clinton did not get the provisions denying aid to
immigrants stricken from the bill, he was able to improve the legislation
considerably (in his opinion) compared to the previous bills that he had
vetoed, the second of which was labeled HR 4. According to the United
States Department of Health and Human Services (1996), the enhance-
ments in the PRWORA were numerous compared to HR 4. The major
ones were:

- Medical coverage (Medicaid) was guaranteed for cash-assistance
  recipients (poor children, people with disabilities, pregnant
  women, the aged, and welfare recipients).
- Funding for child care was increased.
- States could not decrease their own spending on child care, using
  higher levels of federal funds to offset their decreases.
- States with good records of moving people to work from welfare
  could receive extra funding.
- Food stamp expenditures were not capped at 2% growth
  regardless of need increases.
- Funds were not reduced for child welfare, foster care, or adoption
  services.
- A larger contingency fund ($2 billion compared to $1 billion) was
  created to assist states in maintaining their funding levels in case
  of a recession or if they experienced large population increases.
- Child care health and safety laws were preserved.
- Family caps were optional for states rather than required.

In his work to alter the welfare reform bill he signed, Clinton, after his reelection in 1996, focused on restoring cuts to food stamps and restoring aid to legal immigrants. He was successful in both endeavors, strengthening his policy goal achievement.

A problem with the rating of the accomplishments of welfare reform is that there are a number of goals, not all of which can be met simultaneously. While self-sufficiency and lack of dependency are touted as being most important goals in the legislation, the key metrics in most analyses of the 1996 welfare reform law are that the number of recipients declined substantially (even during economic downturns) and that there has been considerable cost savings in welfare spending (Peck and Gershon, 2000). Critics argue that these metrics are misplaced, pointing to research that indicates that large percentages of former welfare recipients continue to have low incomes and that some segments of the poor are worse off now compared to during the AFDC era.

AN ALTERNATIVE VIEW OF THE GOALS OF WELFARE REFORM

One of the more interesting aspects of the rational actor model is the dispute over what the "real" goals of a major player are. It would be remiss of us to accept at face value the stated goals set forth by President Clinton, Senator Lott, and Speaker Gingrich without acknowledging an alternative view of the situation, particularly from feminist and Leftist perspectives. People critiquing Clinton from the political left have been especially vociferous, feeling as though a president from the Democratic Party should not have signed the welfare reform bill he was given by the Republican Congress.

The Leftist critique argues that the main goal of the conservative wing of the Republican Party has been to dismantle the welfare state and make the world safe for capitalism. "As in the past, the most recent reforms have sought to (1) enforce work, (2) promote marriage, and (3) weaken the welfare state. These goals meshed well with the neoliberal plan to shrink the role of government and to raise profits by redistributing income upward from the have-nots to the haves" (Abramovitz, 2006, p. 27).

These goals, the Leftists maintain, played out on a background of racism that painted the "welfare problem" on people of color, particularly African Americans (Abramovitz, 2006; Joseph, 2006; Reisch, 2000).

Critics also viewed welfare reform as part of an effort to regulate women's lives and reproductive choices, based at least on the policies enacted in many states to deny additional funding to families where a child was conceived while the mother was enrolled in the TANF program.

AN ALTERNATIVE VIEW OF THE ACCOMPLISHMENTS OF THE KEY PLAYERS

Blau (2006) places the PRWORA of 1996 in a context that is familiar to students of history. "What has happened in recent social welfare policy hews closely to the historical pattern. In the midst of a transition from one dominant mode of production to another, social welfare policy will usually enforce work norms" (p. 55). Other programs since 1996 have also been targeted to help enforce work norms: unemployment insurance eligibility has been made more stringent, mandatory community-service hours for public housing tenants has been required, employment disablement for alcohol and drug addiction has been eliminated. (Blau, 2006).

If the goal of the elites of society is to eliminate barriers to their control of society, then the welfare reform bill was just part of a larger push for the wealthy to maintain their status. Authors who advance this view use information to support their interpretation, yet their conclusions are not tested rigorously against other ways of seeing the world. The viewpoint is often presented well but, at its extremes, is presented as an uncontestable truth rather than as a set of testable hypotheses that can be supported or disproven.

CONCLUSION

The rational actor model of policy development posits that the key actors, who can be identified, have specific desires that they want to achieve, a clear view of what their options are, and unambiguous information as to how to achieve the highest level of achievement for the least cost. Critics argue that none of these assumptions hold. People do not have a clear hierarchy of desires, they do not really understand all their options, and they cannot predict with certainty that some actions will ultimately lead to better results than other actions. Furthermore, it may be that the goals that are openly espoused are not the "real" goals that the actor is after. Hidden agendas abound, and little can be taken at face value. We have noted that there are both policy and political goals that actors strive to achieve.

Despite these obvious problems, the rational actor model is still frequently used as it is the approach that is most in line with a means–end view of policy; namely, that policy actors are trying to solve problems and choose the most efficient means possible to do so. In general, it can be argued that the fields of program evaluation and policy analysis were started and remain firmly grounded in the rational actor model or its variant, the boundedly rational actor model. Elected officials notice problems, legislation sets forth goals to "do something" about problems, programs attempt to achieve the legislated goals, and evaluation and analysis seek to determine whether those goals were accomplished.

WHAT IS AHEAD

The rest of this book takes a much closer look at the evaluation and analysis of the results of policy. Properly done, evaluation will uncover the outcomes of programs and policies. Some of these outcomes are related to the stated purposes of the policy, while others are not. This second set is frequently called "unanticipated" or "unintended" consequences, although it may be argued that not all of the consequences in this group are unanticipated or unintended at all. They may just be unannounced or undeclared. Because policy creation emerges from the actions of many stakeholders, some of the explicit goals of a law may be contradictory. This is also true of the implicit goals of legislation and shows that comprehensive rationality is difficult to achieve in a group decision-making or political system.

Part II of the book examines the use of qualitative, quantitative, and mixed methods evaluation and provides in-depth examples of studies of welfare reform using them. Each example is analyzed to show its strengths and weaknesses. There is no attempt made to provide an overview or summation of the breadth of welfare reform research. The purpose of the next section is rather to introduce readers to the techniques used by program evaluators so that, in further reading, they will be prepared to understand the choices made in the design and development of research and evaluation, not just of TANF program elements, but of other policies and programs as well.

SUMMARY OF THE THREE MODELS

The preceding three chapters have contained a great deal of information and application. Because of this, readers may find a quick overview of all three models helpful (see Table 4.2).

The first row provides the key source document for the model. The second row lists the questions to ask in order to understand the policy creation process from each model. This set of questions allows the information seeking of the analyst to be systematic and rigorous. Clearly, one can do the research more or less well. Thus, the standards of being "systematic" and "rigorous" are related to one's training and self-motivation to be excellent at the tasks.

The third row shows what each model emphasizes. The emphasis is what differentiates the models from each other. The *historical* model emphasizes continuities of policy debates. This model, for example, asks why the issue has come to the fore at a particular time. This model also asks about similarities and differences between the political context from earlier times and the time being considered.

The *politics and power* model emphasizes the bargaining that takes place between actors with unequal power, positions, and abilities. When it is done thoroughly, the reader will understand what the espoused policy goals are and also what the internal motivations are for these goals. It might be that the policy actor is pursuing an altruistic goal of "making the world a better place." It might be, however, that the policy goal is really more or less part of a larger strategy to achieve a different goal. This other goal may be something such as promoting their own career, gaining control of a legislative body, attacking an enemy, and so forth. Even though the politics and power model begins in much the same way as the historical model, by identifying the relevant actors, their views, and how they define the problem, the point of gathering this information is very different. The historical model examines the long term sweep of things; the power and politics model is mainly short-term and case study–oriented.

Table 4.2 Summary of Three Models

	Historical	*Politics and Power*	*Rational Actor*
Key Source	Spano (2000)	Allison and Zelikow (1999)	Allison and Zelikow (1999)
Questions to Ask	Identify the relevant actors, their areas of contention, and how they define the problem.	*Who* plays? That is, whose views and values count in shaping the choice and action?	What are the goals (desired end states) of the key actors?
	Examine sources to try to understand why the issue is being considered at that particular time in history. Determine if it is a new problem and what specific events may have sparked the policy debate.	What *factors* shape each *player's* (a) perceptions; (b) preferred course of action; and thus (c) the player's stand on the issue?	What are the objective characteristics of the situation?
	Discern the ideology behind the policy positions.	What *factors* account for each player's impact on the choice and action?	How close did the key actors come to getting what they wanted?
	Try to identify similarities and differences in the political context between the social policy conflict under study and previous efforts to address the topic. What may have led to the resurgence of policy debate regarding this topic?	What is the "*action channel*"; that is, the established process for aggregating competing perceptions, preferences, and stands of players in making decisions and taking action?	
Emphasizes	Historical continuities of policy debates	The bargaining that takes place around policy among actors with unequal power, positions, and abilities	The goals of policy and the processes of analysis

(*Continued*)

Table 4.2 continued

	Historical	Politics and Power	Rational Actor
Advantages	Often, considerable source material for recent policies. Straightforward, easy to understand. Places the information into context.	Seems correct to people who "have been there." Promotes clearer understanding of processes used in policy making.	It "works" in many cases to provide helpful understanding. Takes purpose of the actors into account.
Critiques	Generally atheoretical and descriptive. Potential lack of generalizability, validity, and reliability.	A great deal of trouble to get the "inside story." May miss the larger picture by focusing on the "play-by-play."	Cannot be fully accurate, as rationality is always bounded. Ignores reality of collective-action problem and altruism.

The *rational actor* model emphasizes the espoused goals of policy. It assumes that there is a problem, that the policy actors want to solve that problem, and that the policy chosen is among the best ways to solve that problem. In the process, one compares the desired positions of the key actors and the policy chosen. In this way, the model sets up the way to determine whether the policy is effective or not: "Is it meeting the goal?"

The last two rows show the advantages and disadvantages of each model. These rows are important because they show how each model is particularly useful or problematic. Emphasizing the need to match the model chosen with the research questions of interest, the advantages and disadvantages point to the wide range of approaches that social policy analysts need to be aware of, understand, and, to a lesser extent, master. Mastery over one or a few techniques is preferable to trying to be a jack-of-all-trades, and doing none of them well.

Part II

Social Policy Evaluation

Part I of this book examined the idea of social policy creation and asked "How did the policy that is in place come to be?" It discussed three ways to approach understanding the kind of policy that emerged to be implemented. What we found was that the model chosen, consciously or not, guides the way the analyst comes to understand the process and outcome. An historical approach may come across as a set of chronological steps, having no consistent theme or purpose, but setting down the facts as the author has lived or discovered them. An historical approach may also be more thematic, such as seeing welfare reform as part of a larger movement to protect capitalism and increase profits, at a very large-scale level of analysis. The second approach, delving into the politics, power, and personality of the key actors, leads to an institutional and individualistic view of the policy that develops. The third approach, the rational actor model, focuses on individual goals and how best to achieve them.

These models come up with different answers. This is certainly reasonable, given that they ask different questions. The information sources are similar, though the elements chosen to be emphasized are different. Having examined all three approaches we may feel fairly clear about what happened and can move back and forth from one model to the next to fill in gaps that each model leaves unanswered. Each model is a way to simplify the information-gathering process to focus on some things and not others. Yet there is nonetheless a nagging doubt that if we only had access to additional sources, or to deeper psychological studies, or something else that is right around the corner, as yet hidden from our view, we could come up with a better answer. We are stuck, however, in time and have to be content with that. In reality, most analysts of a social policy are not going to go to the trouble of conducting three different studies, following three different models and sets of questions. Time pressures are too intense and staff resources are too limited to expect this to be a common occurrence. The key lesson from Part I is to choose one's approach carefully, for it will determine, to a very large extent, what is produced as an answer.

Part II of this book takes the policy as a given and then asks, "How do we know the policy's effects?" This is a fundamentally different question from how we got this particular policy in the first place. But we find that the wide variety of approaches available to begin to approach the question leads us to question ourselves once more. Researchers and program evaluators have a variety of tools at their disposal, as well as worldviews that determine which research questions they ask and tools they choose. Ideology is an important, if often unexamined, factor, as are the norms of the endeavor. As described by Ron Haskins (2006), a Republican staffer on the House Ways and Means Committee, and an eyewitness to the welfare reform effort, social scientists and politicians view research and evaluation from two opposed perspectives: "Whereas social scientists start with a question and follow strict rules to arrive at an answer, politicians usually start with the answer and use the results of social science—selectively if necessary—to support their predetermined answer . . . using facts correctly that do not provide the entire story is not regarded as particularly heinous in politics" (p. 49). Haskins makes no apology for this but finds it worth mentioning in case his audience does not understand this vital difference in perspective.

Another difference in perspective among social scientists is the proper approach to understanding the effects of policy. This relates to basic views of the world, traceable to an acceptance of an empirically verifiable world external to the observer (positivism and its variants) or to the belief that all of us create our own worlds, based on our own unique life experiences and abilities, and that these particular worlds are all "true" at some level (constructivism). For positivists, evaluation needs to consider changes (or lack of changes) in behaviors and generally should use quantitative measures of attitudes, beliefs, and behaviors. Constructivists, on the other hand, are less likely to be interested in the things that quantitative measures can tell us. Because each person's world is unique, narrative and qualitative methods are used to examine thoughts and ideas, and beliefs and their meanings are most important in understanding policy impacts. Constructivists frequently use the grounded theory research method which builds theory "from data by beginning with observations and looking for patterns, themes, or common categories in those observations" (Rubin and Babbie, 2008, p. 638) and frequently desire to include the viewpoints of the less powerful members of society so that they can be represented in policy debates.

The discussion of differing views can rapidly bog down forward movement. I believe it is a safe generalization that most scholars of social policy now see at least some validity in both viewpoints, and mixed methods (combining quantitative and qualitative methods of data collection) are seen as valuable contributors to an overall understanding of the world.

As we move into the rest of this book, we must be careful as we address the issue of conducting evaluation or research on policy to understand our own views and biases. These differences may be ideological (more liberal vs. more conservative), paradigmatic (more positivist vs. more constructivist), methodological (more quantitative vs. more qualitative) or fall along some other fault line. The view of this book is to try to present all issues in as unbiased a way as possible, recognizing that every author has biases that the reader should take into account. Using multiple sources of information and other resources assists in reducing extreme effects of approaching any topic from only one point of view.

The next chapters examine different research methodologies used in policy analysis, specifically on the effects of the welfare reform law of 1996. Chapter 5 examines qualitative research methods and provides examples of their use. Chapter 6 looks at quantitative methods, issues, and results of evaluations using them. Chapter 7 provides similar information when both qualitative and quantitative methods are used in the same study (mixed methods research).

The amount of evaluative research associated with the PRWORA is enormous and constantly growing. Because of the amount of research that has been conducted and continues to be published, any literature review would be incomplete and out of date before it is finished, much less published. Thus, the decision in this book was made to use illustrative studies in each of these chapters, to emphasize how the choices made by researchers affect their study's quality.

The examples used in the next three chapters were chosen to demonstrate a number of different evaluative questions and the methods chosen to answer them. All of the evaluation write-ups have strengths and imperfections. Evaluations, after all, must balance the needs for systematic and rigorous data-collection processes with the requirement of being timely and policy-relevant within the constraints of a particular budget.

5

Using Qualitative Methods to Understand What the Policy Did

O nce policies have been selected and implemented, social policy analysis can yield to social policy evaluation; that is, determining what happened as a result of the policy. This chapter introduces students to qualitative evaluation methods in a social policy context. Basic methods are illustrated by qualitative evaluations of TANF outcomes.

Qualitative methods, while currently used in almost every area of social science, originated in the fields of anthropology and sociology. Because of the variety and breadth of qualitative methods, this chapter is only a basic overview of key concepts necessary to understand qualitative policy evaluation. This chapter briefly defines qualitative research, describes some of the key qualitative methods used by policy researchers to study the effects of policy, and identifies data collection techniques employed in qualitative policy research. It also discusses the advantages and criticisms of these methods and provides examples of their use in understanding the effects of welfare reform in the United States.

DESCRIPTION OF THE QUALITATIVE APPROACH TO SOCIAL POLICY EVALUATION

The description of the qualitative approach starts with information relating to its *epistemological* foundation, or beliefs about knowledge. The basic question in any social science endeavor is how to "know" something—that is, when we say something is true, how do we know it is true? Researchers committed to a qualitative approach to knowledge-creation align themselves with "an interpretive epistemology that stresses the dynamic, constructed and evolving nature of social reality. In this view, there is no objective science that can establish universal truths or can exist independently of the beliefs, values and concepts created to understand the world" (Devine, 2002, p. 201). In other words, any reality under study "is understood as a complex system that is more than the sum of its parts; focus[ing] on complex interdependencies and system dynamics that cannot meaningfully be reduced to a few discrete variables and linear, cause-effect relationships" (Patton, 2002, p. 41).

SPECIFIC QUALITATIVE RESEARCH METHODS IN SOCIAL POLICY EVALUATION

Most qualitative researchers and evaluators ascribe to interpretivism, which is an approach that "focuses on gaining an empathic understanding of how people feel inside, seeking to interpret individuals' everyday experiences, deeper meanings and feelings, and idiosyncratic reasons for their behaviors" (Rubin and Babbie, 2008, p. 639). Thus, their methods are grounded in naturalistic inquiry "studying real-world situations as they unfold naturally" in "nonmanipulative and noncontrolling" ways with an "openness to whatever emerges (lack of predetermined constraints on findings)" (Patton, 2002, p. 40). Thus, qualitative methods involve both theoretical orientations and data collection techniques.

Qualitative researchers and evaluators choose their theoretical orientations at the beginning of the study, taking into account the goals of the project (Padgett, 2008; Patton, 2002). Theoretical orientations particularly appropriate to social policy analysis include *phenomenology*—the study of the *lived experience* of those impacted by the policy; *grounded theory*—where theories about the policy are developed based on the data collected; *action research*—focusing on social change and empowerment through active partnerships between researchers and community; and *hermeneutics* as presented in Chapter 2 of this text. Because action research is the most in line with social work values, a more in-depth discussion of this theoretical approach follows.

Participatory Action Research/Action Research

According to Kindon, Pain, and Kesby (2007, p. 1), participatory action research (PAR) "involves researchers and participants working together to examine a problematic situation or action to change it for the better." One of the purposes of PAR is to remove the hierarchy of researcher/evaluator and subject and to empower the people who have formerly been subjects of research to become creators and participants in research that is non-coercive, democratically developed, and that affects them directly (Kindon, Pain, and Kesby, 2007). The process of PAR is iterative, with at least one person with training in research methods and a larger group of people who have little prior knowledge or training but who want to participate in the processes of research or evaluation (empower-ment evaluation, as described by Fetterman and Wandersman, [2004], is another example of a similar conceptual framework). Berg (2009) adds that action research is a "highly collaborative, reflective, experiential, and participatory mode of research in which all individuals involved in the study, researcher and subjects alike, are deliberate and contributing actors in the research enterprise" (p. 247).

The process and language of action research is meant to be simple to understand, without lacking rigor. It mimics the learning process, in that the action research process involves three phases: *looking,* or noticing what is going on in one's environment; *thinking,* or interpreting one's observations in context to assess the situation; and *acting,* or doing something that is designed to improve the lives of the people involved (Berg, 2009). Participatory action research demands a set of skills not usually associated with researchers or evaluators of social programs and issues. People who prefer being the "research authority in the room" will find this a poor fit for their style. Berg cautions that the role of a researcher using PAR "must be more holistic, encompassing a broad combination of technological, social, economic and political aspects of relationships and interactions between the researcher and the stakeholders in the project" (2009, p. 258). The purpose of this research approach is to understand and solve concerns of particular people. As such, PAR is not going to provide the basis for testing theoretical models. The results of PAR are also probably not going to be easily extrapolated to other groups or situations (Berg, 2009) although the results may be very useful to the particular situation at the heart of the research.

Design Issues

As qualitative researchers design their studies, though the theoretical approach guides the overall approach to the study, there are norms in terms of design relating to sampling, data collection, and data analysis. Sampling is often a two-phase process where the first phase employs purposive sampling, which is "a deliberate process of selecting respondents based on their ability to provide the needed information" (Padgett, 2008, p. 53). Typically, qualitative researchers will begin with six to ten respondents. During collection and analysis of information gleaned from these respondents, researchers embark on the second phase, theoretical sampling (Padgett, 2008). Theoretical sampling is "sampling on the basis of the emerging concepts, with the aim being to explore the dimensional range or varied conditions along which the properties of concepts vary" (Patton, 2002, p. 490).

Data Collection

Qualitative researchers tend to use a short list of data collection techniques regardless of theoretical approach. A number of authors have set forth descriptions of typical qualitative research data collection techniques. In this chapter, we briefly discuss two of the most relevant: interviewing and focus groups. The purpose here is not so much to turn anyone into a skillful qualitative researcher, but rather to allow the reader of evaluation studies using these techniques to understand what has taken place in the evaluation process to derive the data and information reported. Being exposed to the more common of the qualitative theoretical approaches, data collection and analysis techniques can also lead to questioning the choices of researchers when reading their reports. For example, readers may be led to ask, "Would an action research approach probably have provided different answers to the evaluation question than the use of a more traditional approach to research, such as phenomenology?" "Why did the evaluators use individual interviews to gather data rather than conduct focus groups?" or "Why did the evaluators use grounded theory analysis?"

Interviewing

Interviewing, as a data collection technique, is defined as "a conversation with a purpose" (Berg, 2009, p. 101), with the purpose being to gather information from the interviewee regarding program processes and impact. This is distinguishable from other types of interviews in social work practice, such as interviewing for problem assessment purposes or interviewing as an intervention technique, such as "motivational interviewing," which is defined as "a client-centered, directive method for enhancing motivation to change by exploring and resolving the client's ambivalence" (Walsh and Corcoran, 2006, p. 253).

Research-focused interviewing can be divided into three basic categories, depending on the level of rigidity with which the structure of the interview is presented. The most rigid is the *structured interview*, which has the same questions, worded in the same way, in the same order, with no additions, clarifications, or adjusting of language permitted. "Researchers assume that the questions scheduled in their interview instrument are sufficiently comprehensive to elicit from subjects all (or nearly all) information relevant to the study's topic[s]" (Berg, 2009, p. 105). This type of interviewing is the weakest form of qualitative interviewing, as it does not align with the value that there is *not* one universal and objective reality.

Un-standardized interviews, the other end of the continuum, are heuristic (i.e., conversational), usually with one or two guiding questions to serve as catalysts in the interview process. The interviewer adds questions, provides clarifications and answers respondent questions, and adjusts the language of the questions to fit the interviewee. Central to the choice of using an un-standardized interview is the belief that, because reality is not universal, a researcher cannot develop ahead of time a full list of questions, and the same question may mean different things to different respondents (Patton, 2002).

The final approach, *semi-standardized interviewing*, has characteristics in between the very rigid and the heuristic methods of standardized and un-standardized interviewing. Semi-standardized interviewing can be more or less structured in nature but consists of a more flexible ordering of questions (though most will be asked in some way), less adherence to a particular wording of questions, and more unscheduled follow-up questions or probes to gain additional insight into the respondents' answers (Berg, 2009).

While the structure of the interview is most important, the method of delivery of the interview also requires thought. Several options exist, including face-to-face interviews, telephone interviews, computer-assisted telephone or personal interviews, and web-based interviews. Most qualitative researchers think first of face-to-face interviewing, as it is the easiest way to develop rapport and to be able to pick up nonverbal cues. Face-to-face interviews can be limited to a relatively close set of respondents, however, because the cost of travel to a dispersed group of subjects can be prohibitive.

Telephone interviewing can help with the problem of travel costs considerably, especially with the cost of long-distance phone calls being minimal. Berg (2009) notes that telephone interviewing may be most useful when the researcher and the person being interviewed have already developed a relationship. The wider expanse of territory and the consequent variety of interviewees may make up for the disadvantages of telephone interviewing, particularly the decrease in the amount of nonverbal information that the evaluator can receive. However, this disadvantage to the telephone interview may dissipate over time with the advent of video calling. Interviewing via telephone, with or without video calling, may at times decrease the number of certain populations who can be reached, however. People without telephones are without a doubt excluded. Other categories of people are likely to self-select out of even random calling efforts through the use of caller ID technology.

Computers can be used to assist telephone-based qualitative interviewing efforts. One of the best approaches is to use the computer to provide the text of what the interviewer is to ask while also recording the conversation for later transcription and entry into the data analysis software. This technique is termed *computer assisted telephone interviewing* (CATI). Taking this type of effort one step further, while retaining a face-to-face mode, is *computer assisted personal interviewing* (CAPI). With the advent of web cameras available for and often integrated into computers, and video capture software, entire conversations in front of a camera can be recorded for later analysis, and distance becomes much less of a problem for gaining access to people to interview. One final type of interviewing that uses computer technology is *computer assisted self-administered interviewing*, or CASI. This has been used both as a modern version of a self-administered paper and pencil survey, and as an audio-based survey, where the respondent can hear the questions read and reply orally, with the computer recording the exact language and intonations used in answering.

The current frontiers of computer assisted interviewing are not limited to personal computers but reach into the World Wide Web. Internet-based surveys using open-ended questions are easy to create and can serve some of the same needs as other types of interviews. Technology such as this shows promise, but of course has its costs also, financially as well as in terms of respondent–interviewer rapport. Many of the people who could provide invaluable information via interviews of any type may be less comfortable with or used to technology than are university-based evaluators or researchers who use this tool frequently.

Focus groups

A focus group is a face-to-face interview of a small group of people to gather information on a particular topic of interest to the group members and the researcher. Focus groups may at first appear to be an easy way to interview a number of people at one time, but the proper use of focus group techniques includes the dynamics and interactions of the group members as part of the information collected (Berg, 2009). Frequently used in marketing studies, focus groups have the potential to elicit opinions, ideas, beliefs, and impressions that are then commented on by other members of the group. Focus groups are typically made up of people who are rather similar to each other so as to encourage a sense of camaraderie and alikeness. These feelings, in turn, may lead to a greater willingness to be open and sharing about the topics of discussion, which are introduced by a focus group leader or moderator (who may or may not be the researcher behind the evaluation). Focus groups' purposes can be varied, and they can best be used in the following ways:

- obtain basic information from group members;
- generate hypotheses for later research;
- stimulate new, creative ideas through participant interaction;
- diagnose problems with a program or idea;
- obtain impressions from participants;

- learn the language used by members of the group to discuss particular topics, which can then feed into the wording of questions in later research efforts; and
- assist in understanding of other research results (Berg, 2009, pp. 158–159, after Stewart and Shamdasani, 1990, p. 15).

Their versatility is one of their strengths. Another plus of focus groups is the ability to develop new insights, based on the participation of even the small number of people in a typical group. Because the moderator allows and encourages spontaneous thinking about only a few topics, the concentrated energy of a focus group can be remarkable.

On the less positive side, the usefulness of the results of a focus group depends largely on the skill level of the moderator. Too much guidance, or too little, and the group can grow quiet and resentful, or veer off-course to areas of no interest to the evaluation (Royce, Thyer, and Padgett, 2010). Additionally, depending upon politics and the nature of the members' relatedness to each other, the focus group setting may actually stifle unpopular or unique perspectives on the topic of focus, providing a skewed data set to the researcher. As is true of the choice of any particular research method, the purpose and resources of the project must take precedence over other concerns (except ethics).

Data analysis

Data analysis is an iterative (ongoing) process, from the beginning of data collection through the final reporting of results. Numerous approaches to qualitative data analysis exist, but one of the most common is grounded theory (GT) (Padgett, 2008). "GT entails inductive coding from the data, memo writing to document analytic decisions, and weaving in theoretical ideas and concepts without permitting them to drive or constrain the study's emergent findings" (Padgett, 2008, p. 32). Grounded theory is not an easy process to describe briefly, and the goal here is not to prepare students to be grounded theorists but rather to summarize the GT process for data analysis. In GT, codes or concepts are identified (open coding) then organized into categories or themes (axial coding). During axial coding, constant comparison is used across sources of data (e.g., transcripts of interviews and focus groups, content analysis of policies, observations of policy implementation) to organize codes into the categories and themes. It is not uncommon during axial coding to uncover new open codes. Also, it is during the axial coding phase that theoretical sampling usually occurs, which will inevitably lead to new open codes and perhaps new axial codes. These axial codes are then interpreted into some description, framework, or relational statements of the phenomenon being studied (Padgett, 2008; Patton, 2002).

Trustworthiness of research

There are certain measures qualitative researchers take to enhance the trustworthiness of their research (Patton, 2002). These measures are necessary given the philosophical underpinnings of qualitative research. Qualitative research is a daunting task since the understanding is that there are multiple realities or interpretations of reality that affect how a phenomenon is experienced. The qualitative researcher has the task of capturing each unique reality or interpretation and then analyzing these to identify the commonalities. Of course, with such a process, there are many possibilities for sampling bias, over- or under-interpretation, and researcher bias. Sampling bias is of great concern considering the norm of using purposeful sampling in qualitative research. However, theoretical sampling as a second layer to the process is the mechanism employed for addressing this issue (Padgett, 2008). Once theoretical sampling is implemented to ensure the uncovering of various realities or interpretations, the activities of the researcher with making sense of the data are the next horizons where trustworthiness must be ensured, usually through triangulation and transparency.

Triangulation

Triangulation can happen in a number of ways, some easier than others. The most common is triangulation of sources, where the data are derived from multiple sources. Though the most common, this requires planning prior to the analysis phase (Patton, 2002). For example, a qualitative policy analysis may involve interviews with members of the people affected by the policy as well as interviews with personnel who have to enact the policies. Both of these sources have an independent view of, for example, the effects of a change in welfare policy. Staff may focus on the resistance of clients to looking for work, while clients may focus on the lack of flexibility in the new program and the way new rules do not take their specific needs into account. Understanding both viewpoints gives the evaluator and the ultimate consumer of the report a better grasp of the effects of the change in policy.

Another type of triangulation is that of methods, also a type that must be planned before data analysis. Methods triangulation involves using more than one data collection technique and can be solely qualitative or can span into mixed methods (Patton, 2002), which are discussed in Chapter 7. For example, in a policy analysis, interviews may be one method used for data collection, along with survey research—a quantitative technique discussed in Chapter 6. This type of multiple methods of information gathering provides greater depth to the quantitative data and gives broader meaning to the qualitative accounts.

Triangulation of analysts is highly desirable as it provides a "checks-and-balances" system for the researcher. With triangulation of analysts, the researcher invites other experts (either in qualitative technique or the topic studied) to review the data and confirm or negate the researcher's various findings (Patton 2002). A stronger, more desirable form of this type of triangulation is the member check. With member checks, the researcher presents interpretations of the participants' realities to the participants themselves for confirmation, critique, and revision. This type of triangulation often helps a researcher suppress biases and not overlook things that might seem obvious to him or her because of the closeness to the topic. The final and least-used type of triangulation is that of theory. This involves the researcher's using more than one theoretical approach for the study (Patton, 2002). For example, an evaluator might use both phenomenology and participatory action research to both capture the lived experience of the subjects and to empower them to change their realities.

Transparency

The primary instrument in qualitative research is the researcher, as the data are collected by this person and then filtered through him or her in the data analysis process. "The principle is to report any personal and professional information that may have affected the data collection, analysis, and interpretation" (Patton, 2002, p. 566).Considering the tremendous number of opportunities the researcher has for interpreting the participants' realities through his or her own lens, an important aspect of any qualitative research report should be information about the researcher. This should include experience and training related to qualitative research and to the topic studied and who funded the research, and how access was gained to the study site (e.g., "Is there a particular relationship with the site that might lead to bias?").

ADVANTAGES OF THE QUALITATIVE APPROACH TO SOCIAL POLICY EVALUATION

Researchers and evaluators are exhorted to match their research techniques to the questions they are trying to answer. Thus, any advantages of the qualitative (or quantitative and mixed) approach are inherently relative to what might occur if one had chosen a different technique. Consider, for example, a do-it-yourself homeowner faced with a hammer and a screwdriver. Both might solve the problem of getting two pieces of wood to stay together. Yet, in the particular instance at hand, the homeowner might prefer using a screwdriver and a screw, or the better solution might be a hammer and nail. Thus it is that an evaluator may be able to choose a qualitative method or a quantitative one, and should choose the one that is most likely to achieve the desired end of the project. (Even highly educated evaluators need to be careful of the reality of the adage, "When you have a hammer in your hand, everything looks like a nail," so that they consciously choose the most appropriate techniques.)

Qualitative techniques of inquiry are sometimes said to be most appropriate in certain situations, such as when not much is known regarding the subject. This can come across as a bit condescending by those judging the issue. After all, the argument is, if we do not know much about the topic and cannot bring "real" research techniques to bear, then it is all right to start the discovery process using these inferior qualitative techniques. Another time that qualitative techniques have particular value is in helping researchers better understand quantitative results. This situation shows the value of bringing individual recipients' views out to illustrate what a set of dry numbers may not present well.

Qualitative research is also viewed as the best option when the researcher wants to create an in-depth understanding of the information provider. This takes a great deal of time to accomplish, but is ideal when the individual case is theoretically important as an illustration of larger patterns.

CRITIQUES OF THE QUALITATIVE APPROACH TO SOCIAL POLICY EVALUATION

While there may be considerable agreement (if not unanimity) that qualitative research is appropriate for some research or evaluation questions, a number of criticisms of these methods still circulate. The ones we cover here are typical criticisms, including issues of representativeness, generalizability, reliability, objectivity, and interpretation. One of the problems that qualitative evaluators face in these types of discussions is that positivists using quantitative methods set the terms of the debate. As these typical criticisms are presented, the accompanying qualitative terminology and definitions will be presented along with strategies employed in qualitative research to ensure the trustworthiness of the research.

Representativeness

The concept of *representativeness* is that the sources of information actually in the research (which are not the entire universe of possible sources) are nonetheless similar to the entire possible universe of sources. This is generally only possible to ascertain with any degree of certainty if the researcher has a complete list of all possible sources before selecting any of them. In most cases, evaluators choosing qualitative methods do not have a list of the entire universe of possible sources. This is often because of the newness of the topic of study or the difficulty in reaching potential subjects of the study. (While this occurs in quantitative evaluations as well, different methods are used to overcome this problem than in evaluations using qualitative methods.)

In qualitative research, the primary strategy employed is that of theoretical purposive sampling as described previously in this chapter. This allows the researcher to continue to select participants until saturation and redundancy are accomplished. Saturation is reached when various themes have emerged in the data and no new themes emerge with subsequent participants. Redundancy can be accomplished a number of ways, but one of importance to this discussion is that of redundancy of characteristics of participants. This ensures that, as saturation of themes is reached, the likelihood of overlooking new themes is vastly reduced, considering that there is a wide variety of participant characteristics.

Faced with the situation of difficulty in reaching potential subjects, the researcher might also turn to a technique known as "snowball" sampling. Starting with one qualified source, the evaluator asks for additional potential sources who might be willing to provide information. Branching off this way to recruit additional sources allows the researcher to reach interviewees who might otherwise have been unwilling to talk to someone in authority. For example, if an evaluator wanted to learn about people on welfare working "off the books" to obtain additional income without reporting it, very few people breaking the law in this way would be likely to admit to such behavior. But, once one respondent has admitted to illegal behavior and suffered no harm from the admission, that informant might be willing to provide the name of a friend who "might do the same thing"—and this friend might be willing to talk because of the referral.

In qualitative research, the question of representativeness is difficult to consider in a convincing way and perhaps even inappropriate to consider. Given the philosophical stance that there are multiple realities, with diversity in characteristics, settings, situations, and circumstances, and the added layer of how these elements interact, it is difficult to fathom how to arrive at representativeness. What qualitative research studies can provide is an interpretation of how, for example, the policy affects the group studied, given their characteristics, setting, situation, and circumstances. Once several studies of different groups, characteristics, settings, situations, and circumstances are conducted, a *meta-synthesis*, defined as "the bringing together of findings on a chosen theme, the results of which should, in conceptual terms, be greater than the sum of the parts" (Campbell et al., 2003, p. 672), could be conducted to ascertain similarities across those reports and studies.

External Generalizability

External generalizability is the idea that one can take the results one has found and apply them to different people at different locations or at different times; that is, one can say the results would be similar regarding people who were outside of the original study. External generalizability is closely linked to the representativeness of the sources of information and to the positivist philosophy that there is one objective reality. If the sources are randomly selected from the entire possible population of interest, it is assumed that the results are nearly always representative and thus generalizable. Given the difficulty in having representative sampling in qualitative research efforts, it is thus also difficult to have a strong claim that the results of the study apply to more than just the people in the study. Thus, one may learn a great deal about a few individuals. An additional difficulty with applying the positivist concept of external generalizability to qualitative research is that qualitative researchers do not ascribe to the philosophy that there is one objective reality to be applied beyond the study participants.

Schofield (1990) contends that the concept of generalizability in qualitative evaluation has become much more important and that "generalizability is best thought of as a matter of the 'fit' between the situation studied and others to which one might be interested in applying the concepts and conclusions of that study" (p. 230). Qualitative researchers typically refer to this as *transferability* or *extrapolation*. For this reason, qualitative researchers and evaluators are exhorted, in addition to theoretical sampling and the search for saturation and redundancy, to give "thick," rich descriptions of both their study participants and the study situation, setting, and circumstances. This assists the consumers of the research in making their own decisions about whether the people they are working with are close enough in characteristics, situation, setting, and circumstances to have the results transferred or extrapolated to them (Patton, 2002).

Reliability

Reliability is the idea that the researcher, or another researcher using the same technique, would obtain a similar answer if the question being asked were asked again. A common example of reliability in research texts is that of a scale, which tells you that you weigh the same if you step off, and then back on. A reliable research effort is valuable, even if it 'is not exactly correct, because you can ascertain movement and trends across the data. You might not know the exact score of an instrument, but you can still tell if things are getting worse or better. Reliability is important in conducting quantitative research. Researchers using quantitative techniques strive to develop studies that can be replicated by other researchers and yield similar results. Reliability is routinely reported in quantitative findings and contributes to the overall quality and credibility of the research. On the other hand, reliability is not appropriate to judging qualitative research, as it is not in agreement with the philosophical underpinnings of qualitative methodology. Qualitative research is grounded in the philosophy that there is not one objective reality. Qualitative researchers argue all individuals have their own reality, shaped by their personal beliefs and experiences. Qualitative methodology is premised on allowing data to emerge through the perspective of the participants, focusing on maintaining the integrity of the individual's reality. Given this, to seek similar answers to questions across different samples is not compatible with qualitative research.

Objectivity/Confirmability

Objectivity in research is predicated on the ability observe the subject of the research or evaluation without having an emotional involvement in what the results are. Objectivity is essentially a positivist concept and one that is considered irrelevant to qualitative studies (Yanow, 2006a). According to Devine (2002), "qualitative researchers neither subscribe to the view that research can be objective, nor do they seek objectivity in field relations" (p. 206). The goal of objectivity—that is, that policy assessors can look at a policy's effects on people with no feelings on their part—is not germane to the purpose of qualitative scholars. Objectivity is a goal of a different system—as much to say to a pagan that her religion will not get her to heaven. If there is no heaven to get to (in the pagan's worldview), then the entire matter is irrelevant. Lincoln and Guba (1985) provide a term more suited to their concepts of qualitative methods: *confirmability*. If something can be confirmed, then there is a bit of a sense of objectivity to its existence because others can also determine its existence.

From an evaluation standpoint, the idea of confirmability is important. Readers and funders of the program and evaluation will be interested in understanding the steps taken to ensure that researcher bias is not tainting the results to such an extreme that others would not recognize the information presented as true. Sadler (1981) catalogues

13 processes that lead to bias in judgment, grouped into three categories: ethical compromises, background experience, and limitations in information-processing abilities inherent to humans. Thus, it is useful to build in safeguards to reduce unconfirmable conclusions. This is achieved primarily through triangulation of analysts and the transparency of the researcher (Patton, 2002), as described previously in this chapter. If objectivity is impossible to attain, it is better to acknowledge that subjectivity prevails and has an effect on the evaluation being conducted, and then take that bias into account as one digests the results of the report.

Interpretation

All research and evaluation involves the interpretation of the information (data) that has been collected. The question is not whether interpretation of data exists or not, but rather the grounds for believing that a particular interpretation is "plausible" at some sort of basic level or, at a higher level of argument, that the interpretation is "*more* plausible" than other possible interpretations. In this way, the data do not speak for themselves at any time; rather they are like an unknown language, the meaning of which is translated by interpreters (the researchers/evaluators). As we know from comparing two or more English translations of works originally created in another language, the new English language texts, while starting from the same source, are typically not the same. Nuances abound in language, and qualitative researchers try to maintain a sense of nuance in their interpretations. The discussion revolves around when interpretation occurs and how to judge different interpretations for their "truthfulness."

Yanow (2006b) argues that interpretation happens at four separate times in a research study. The first time is in the mind of the person (who might be the evaluator) experiencing the situation of interest (such as an interaction with a TANF employment specialist as opposed to an AFDC eligibility worker). The second time is when the researcher communicates with a person who experienced the event (if any such person exists). In this way, the experience becomes "secondhand," and the interpretive challenges increase. Over time, no person is alive who experienced the situation firsthand, and so documents and other sources become profoundly important. Yanow adds two more interpretive moments: when the study results are being written and new insights are possibly being added, and when the study results are read. Clearly, the more moments of interpretation there are, the more different paths can be taken. Even with just two options at each of the four moments, the number of different interpretations grows quickly, to 16 separate interpretive paths.

What positivists might term as "validity" in interpretation is increased when the qualitative approach demonstrates internal consistency within the data (triangulation of sources and methods, saturation and redundancy of themes), and when independent observers understand the events in the same or similar ways (triangulation of analysts).

USING QUALITATIVE METHODS IN RESEARCHING TANF OUTCOMES

It has been repeated often that the 1996 welfare reform act was the largest change in American welfare policy in 60 years. In the short-term aftermath of the implementation of welfare reform, when not much was known about the subject, one might expect to see a relatively large number of qualitative studies being conducted. According to researchers at the Institute for Research on Poverty (2005).

> Qualitative researchers have used a wide range of data collection strategies, including, but not limited to short interviews, in-depth interviews, life history interviews, focus groups, ethnographic observation, shadowing, time diaries, and mapping. They have analyzed data for thematic content and cultural models, used techniques of narrative analysis, and conducted case-oriented comparative analysis (Institute for Research on Poverty, 2005, Current Qualitative Research).

In addition to all the differences in methods noted by the Institute for Research on Poverty, the number of settings that research could take place in is potentially vast. A final source of variation to think about is the object of study: we can examine the effects of welfare reform on clients, staff, nonprofit organizations, state agencies, neighborhoods and communities, other policies, and even the macroeconomic system.

This section presents some examples of qualitative evaluation research related to welfare reform. Again, this chapter is far too short to provide an overview of all that has been done and the results. The first example examines the perceptions of individual clients; the second example looks at the impact of welfare reform on the involvement of faith-based organizations in service provisions to welfare recipients (Charitable Choice).

Each example will be discussed in terms of its background and research objective, the methods used, and its results and conclusions. It will also be analyzed to determine how well the research demonstrated trustworthiness. The purpose of analyzing these examples is to provide a "hands-on" experience with what other evaluators and researchers are doing, how they are doing it, and what a critically aware reader should be observing about the research efforts.

Example 1:

S. Butler, J. Corbett, C. Bond, and C. Hastedt (2008): Long-term TANF participants and barriers to employment: A qualitative study in Maine. *Journal of Sociology and Social Welfare, 35*(3): 49–69.

Background and Research Objectives
This example manuscript is printed in an academic journal, which therefore presents some limitations to the authors. First, the number of pages that are allowed for the manuscript make it shorter than might be ideal to completely present the methodology and results. Because of length limitations for any one article, authors sometimes break down large-scale research efforts into relatively short and very focused journal manuscript submissions. Thus, a great deal of the "thick description" that qualitative research is known for must be stripped out. These facts about journal articles may help explain the difficulty in finding sufficient information about qualitative research efforts for the characteristics discussed in this chapter.

In discussing the background to this research, the authors indicate that they had a political agenda to counteract particular bills that had been introduced into the Maine legislature that would place harsher requirements on TANF recipients than were currently in place. The research question to be answered was what were the experiences of long-term TANF recipients who "confronted obstacles to becoming employed in Maine" (Butler et al., 2008, p. 54).

> In order to address the stereotypes driving the proposed Maine bill, the staff of Maine Equal Justice Partners (MEJP), an advocacy organization

for low-income individuals and families in Maine, initiated an effort to collect evidence from current recipients of TANF who faced multiple barriers to employment (Butler et al., 2008, p. 51).

Research questions related to:

1. Participants' reasons for first applying for TANF;
2. Their experiences with ASPIRE (Maine's welfare-to-work program) and meeting work requirements;
3. The barriers they perceived to leaving TANF and becoming economically self-sufficient;
4. Their hopes for the future (i.e., what they would like for themselves and their families in five years); and
5. Their perceptions regarding how the public views TANF and the people receiving it (Butler et al., 2008, p. 55).

In this review, we look primarily at the results regarding Question 3, the perceived barriers to leaving TANF and becoming economically self-sufficient.

Methods and Data Collection Techniques Used
The Maine Equal Justice Partners and a university-affiliated researcher conducted the study, leading to policy-relevant information being collected, analyzed, and reported to Maine legislators and residents. This is definitely an example of participatory action research, with its inherent advantages and disadvantages. The authors state that information was collected from 28 women living in Maine through three focus groups and six telephone interviews. Respondents who faced barriers to employment were recruited using the MEJP network and were invited to participate in regional focus groups. These volunteers ($n = 22$) came from the central part of Maine, so additional respondents ($n = 6$) from the northern and southern parts of Maine were recruited for telephone interviews. The focus groups were each about one hour long, while the phone interviews each lasted about 20 minutes. These interactions were guided by the questions noted above. These sessions and individual interviews were recorded and transcribed verbatim, and were then "analyzed for recurring themes using the open-coding process of grounded theory analysis" (Butler et al., 2008, p. 55).

Results and Conclusions

Results of the information gathered from these women in Maine indicate that three major barriers exist: the impact of domestic violence in their lives, the time it takes to care for children with disabilities, and their own health problems (Butler et al., 2008). Many of the women faced more than one of the barriers, and had to deal with other problems, including lack of or unreliable transportation, a lack of available jobs, and a scarcity of proper childcare.

The state of Maine recognizes the difficult situation that women living in abusive situations face in becoming self-sufficient and so has instituted what are known as "good cause" exemptions for the requirements to work for TANF recipients (this is similar to the Family Violence Option [FVO] in the PRWORA at the federal level). Unfortunately, "the experiences reported by women in this study indicate that not all case workers are fully implementing the good cause exemption in Maine" (Butler et al., 2008, p. 65).

The authors of the study are happy to be able to report that, in the end, the bill they were against, and that caused them to begin their research, did not pass. Despite this victory, there is always the possibility that legislators in the next session will introduce similar or even harsher legislation.

Analyzing the Study

The study just described is one of the hundreds that could have been chosen to illustrate the use of qualitative methods regarding some aspect of the 1996 welfare reform law. It was chosen because its research question focused on the life of women facing more stringent work requirements, just as the original recipients of TANF faced a conservative policy change. In the case of Maine, however, the proposed changes were defeated. This manuscript clearly shows the use of research in the political sphere—it was designed and completed quickly in order to be timely and to have policy relevance. So far, none of the client quotes that are in the manuscript have been reproduced here. Reading the statements made by clients provides a great deal more impact than the above synopsis. Here is part of a quote from an aid recipient who left an abusive relationship but did not have her own car:

> How can you get a job if you don't have a vehicle? You're supposed to walk [your child] to childcare, drop him off, hitchhike to work, work

eight hours, come back, get your kid. If you're 15 minutes late it's going to cost you more. . . . It's not worth it, so you either go back to your abuser or you go and live with somebody that you don't know, or whatever, or get a nice big cardboard box to set up underneath a bridge, you know (Butler et al., 2008, pp. 56-7).

The power of qualitative research reports is that they can carry the emotional content of the research "subjects," forcing us to view them as human beings, not "objects of study." Still, there are better and worse models of qualitative methods used in evaluation and policy research. Let us examine this in terms of representativeness, extrapolation, trustworthiness, objectivity/confirmability and interpretation.

Representativeness

The idea of representativeness as achieved through theoretical sampling, redundancy, and saturation is important because it demonstrates that the experiences presented are redundant across a variety of respondents' lives. If the information in the report does not demonstrate saturation and redundancy, then readers may doubt the importance of addressing the issues raised. If almost all of the clients in a population feel as though they are being treated harshly by program staff, for example, that may lead to a very different response than if this were felt by only one or two clients, no matter how strongly those atypical clients felt they were being maltreated.

In this study, the representativeness of the clients interviewed is suspect, for several reasons. First, all of the people in the focus groups and one-on-one interviews were self-selected. Notifications were sent out by the advocacy organization, MEJP, to people who were "current recipients of TANF who faced multiple barriers to employment" (Butler et al., 2008, p. 51). The odds are that people having the most problems are the ones most likely to come forward to express their concerns.

Another way this self-selection occurred is that the advocacy organization, MEJP, already on record as being against the legislation, recruited them. It is a fair guess that women who had already moved off TANF (despite facing barriers) or women who did not have severe problems such as those discussed in this research, were not put into a focus group or interviewed via telephone. Echoing the words of Ron Haskins as he discussed the Republicans' use of incomplete information about the time length of AFDC receipt (Haskins, 2006), this time the liberals were choosing to gather information from women with the most difficult circumstances, not the most typical. The purpose of the research described in this article was not to paint a complete picture, but rather to make the best possible case against the legislation. A complete study should perhaps have included *former* clients who were able to leave TANF despite facing barriers to employment. The experiences of this comparison group would have been very interesting to readers to determine how others have dealt with similar barriers.

Representativeness was also compromised by the geographical distribution of the interviewees, although the research staff moved beyond Maine's larger cities to talk with women in areas in the north and south of the state. The report provides some demographic data about the respondents but does little to show how these women were typical or atypical of the larger population of interest. The respondents seem to have been on TANF much longer (over five years, on average) than average recipients, who were on TANF for less than one year. The longer time on welfare is related, the authors state, to their facing of particular obstacles to leaving the programs. While this group in the research may have many problems, there is no comparison information available to indicate that other current TANF recipients, or former recipients, have fewer of the problems discussed. Also, persons of color or minority status were over-represented in the study population compared to the state averages. Finally, the researchers did not use theoretical sampling to capture the experiences of a wide range of women with the goal of saturation and redundancy. To use 28 volunteer focus group and individual interviewees with such atypical characteristics to represent what is occurring in all of the state is difficult to accept. It seems as though the purpose of the research was not to be representative at all, but to present "worst case scenarios" of what women were facing. Had the researchers included respondents representing both the typical and atypical scenarios for recipients, they would have been able to paint a clearer picture of whether these women's experiences were functions of their atypical characteristics or of flaws in the policy.

Extrapolation

The degree to which it is possible to take the results from this study and apply them to other populations is very much in doubt. Still, just as the researchers did not seem too concerned with showing the typical case through theoretical sampling, saturation, and redundancy, but rather were intent on protecting women with the most extreme cases, the idea of extrapolation does not seem to be much on the authors' minds. One limitation that has been noted about participatory action research is that extrapolation is a very low priority, if it is thought of at all. The key aspect of PAR is to be working with the stakeholders to understand and address a problem.

Trustworthiness through Triangulation and Transparency

Trustworthiness Trust, meaning that researchers have sufficiently employed triangulation and transparency to demonstrate that different researchers would come to similar conclusions when looking at the data in this study, is not at a particularly high level, since much is missing from the write-up. Although the MEJP project utilized triangulation of sources and data collection techniques, there are possible weaknesses in triangulation of analysts related to "the help of a social sciences researcher to assist in the collection, analysis, and presentation of data" (Butler et al., 2008, p. 51). The write-up does not say if this person conducted all the research effort by herself or triangulated with colleagues and the respondents themselves through member checks. Transparency is another issue of great concern. Because the researcher had worked with the group previously, there is a chance that the researcher's interpretations would be quite biased and in line with the ideological position of the advocacy group. This becomes quite important if we believe that the researcher did not use others to code data, test ideas about themes in the transcripts against, and so on.

Objectivity/Confirmability

The authors state that the research was intended to show the barriers that exist for women on TANF (Butler et al., 2008, p. 51): Not to ask *if* barriers exist, but to show the barriers that *do* exist. The desired answers were already known, but it was up to the researcher to see the extent to which they were true. Because of the ideological nature of the research effort, it becomes difficult to agree with the ideas proposed because they seem so predetermined. This is disconcerting, as an aim of qualitative research is to identify realities with the world view that the researcher does not know the realities of the respondents. It leaves one to wonder if the respondents were not led to answer certain ways in how the interviews were conducted and the focus groups were facilitated.

Still, the article attempts to provide some notion of objectivity and confirmability at one point, by including information regarding barriers faced by women in other parts of the United States. The authors are thus able to show that the figures in Maine were not out of line with what has been found elsewhere under welfare reform laws. Barriers found to make obtaining work difficult in other states seem to be found in Maine as well. Using the literature in this way tends to make the results seem more objective—that the potential bias of the researchers did not play a large part in presenting the information.

Interpretation

The analysis of interpretation of the information provided here follows Yanow's (2006b) ideas of the moments when interpretation takes place. First, there is the experience that the members of the study group (long-term TANF clients with multiple problems) had in dealing with their TANF caseworkers specifically and their lives in general. The quotes from clients indicate that their lives were stressful and full of challenges. Choices seemed limited and, in many cases, none of the options were palatable. For example, is it better to move back in or stay with an abusive partner or to struggle alone day after day with myriad problems caused by lack of transportation, providing care for a child with disabilities, and frequently having problems with one's own health?

The second interpretive moment occurred as the focus groups and telephone interviews took place. While the write-up does not make it clear how many researchers conducted the focus groups and telephone interviews, it may be that they were all run by the same person. If this is true, then the interpretation may have been quite similar. If different researchers conducted the interviews, the interpretations of the interactions may be quite different. It does seem that all the researchers shared a common belief, which is that the women in the study are more worthy than society as a whole gives them credit for. Thus, all of the answers provided will be heard with considerable sympathy, and the researchers will want to try to keep the respondents' lives from becoming any bleaker than they already are.

Interpretive moment three occurred when the authors developed the manuscript for publication. Not only were the ideas generated regarding structure, wording, and what to put in and what to leave out, but all this was filtered through the lead author's experiences in writing for academic journals—what is acceptable and what is not within that context. Already mentioned is manuscript length, but also writing style and level of detachment are important elements of academic journal article writing. Interpretive moment four is when readers interact with the written word and interprets it for themselves. In this case, it appears that the information collected and presented to legislators was effective in stopping a particular legislative agenda because it felt like an authentic experience—women on TANF for long periods of time are at least somewhat difficult to move to the paid workforce.

If we were to use a scorecard for these analytical sections, we would see that representativeness is medium, at best; extrapolation is not very good, trustworthiness is weak, objectivity/confirmability is low, and interpretation may seem unfocused. In short, while the results seem mostly true for the women in the study, there is little doubt that these women may be suffering from severe and atypical situations. While the results were useful to allow the advocates to make their point that the women who were long-term recipients of TANF were not "lazy," the study does not meet most standards of rigor as understood by both qualitative and quantitative researchers.

Example 2:

J. Orr (2000): Faith-based organizations and welfare reform: California religious community capacity study: Qualitative findings and conclusions. Los Angeles: Center for Religion and Civic Culture, University of Southern California.

Background and Research Objectives
Unlike Example 1, which was a journal article, this example is a report published by an academic study center. As such, it can presumably be of any length or style, subject to the author's desires to delve into the details of the project.

One of the goals of the welfare reform act, according to Senator John Ashcroft, was to assist in the integration of faith-based organizations into the service-provider network for persons leaving welfare. Senator Ashcroft inserted language into the 1996 law along these lines because he believed that religiously based charities had unfairly been denied access to government funds since the start of the Social Security system in the 1930s (Orr, 2000). In order to determine if this policy goal of the PRWORA was being achieved, a study was funded by the James Irvine Foundation. The primary objective for this study was "to estimate the will and the capacity of California's faith-based organizations to expand their social service outreach in support of welfare-to-work participants" (Orr, 2000, p. 10) in California. This study objective is in line with a rational actor approach to social policy evaluation—if the sponsor of provisions in the law says that the provisions mean something specific, then it is reasonable to test whether that portion of the law is achieving the stated goal.

In order to limit the study as well as focus on the main aspects of the knowledge to be gathered, 11 questions were asked in the research/evaluation. They were:

1. What is Charitable Choice?
2. Does California's "strict church-state separationist" constitution raise problems concerning Charitable Choice that are unique to this state?
3. Has the California legislature supported Charitable Choice?
4. Which faith-based social services qualify for welfare-to-work contract and voucher support?
5. What is the structure of faith-based organizations that offer social services?
6. Are state and county welfare agency administrators encouraging faith-based organizations to participate in welfare-to-work programs?
7. Are California's religious leaders encouraging faith-based organizations to participate in welfare-to-work programs?
8. How are faith-based organizations responding to welfare reform within the Center for Religion and Civic Culture's "Case Study Neighborhoods?"
9. What is the profile of faith-based welfare-to-work contracts that have been funded by federal and state programs?

10. What disincentives affect the willingness of faith-based programs to compete for welfare-to-work contracts?

11. What factors expand the capacity of faith-based organizations to participate in welfare-to-work programs? (Orr, 2000, p. 12).

For this example, we will not cover all the answers to all the questions, but it is interesting to see what the evaluation process of this element of the PRWORA was in California's implementation of national welfare reform principles, called CalWORKs (the California Work Opportunity and Responsibility for Kids program). An interesting angle on welfare reform is the entire issue of how well the program is implemented, or in what ways were the ideas behind the legislation put into practice, not just in the 50 states, but also in the 3,141 counties and parishes in the country, many of which have great latitude in how they handle state and national law enforcement. California is no different from other states in this regard, as the welfare departments in each county have considerable latitude in the way they choose to conceptualize and implement Charitable Choice provisions of welfare reform within the legal mandates and opportunities of California and the United States.

Methods and Data Collection Techniques Used

According to Orr (2000), this evaluation was conducted using qualitative methods, at different levels of the intervention (neighborhood, county and state); specific information on which method (e.g., grounded theory, phenomenology, PAR) was not provided, though information on how researchers were trained indicates ethnographic and phenomenological undertones. Orr indicates that open-ended interviews and participant observations were the primary data-collection techniques used. Interviewers and participant observers were trained and given guides, although these guides were sometimes updated to take into account the information that was leading to new understanding of the situation— a common practice in qualitative research. The data-gathering process was fairly open and unstructured in terms of sources of information ("the Internet, newspapers, journals, professional association meetings, state and county documents, ecumenical and interfaith events, conferences, newsletters, and informal conversations" [Orr, 2000, p. 13]) and in terms of question wording and probes, following a heuristic or conversational style where: "Researchers were instructed to 'follow their stories'; i.e., to follow-up on leads in interviews and observations that promised to reveal previously unanticipated complexities. Individuals who were interviewed were allowed considerable freedom to speak about their personal and organizational responses to welfare reform" (Orr, 2000, p. 13). Participant observers and interviewers at the neighborhood level had to get to know "their" neighborhood, visiting it often, interviewing not only the leaders of religious institutions but also the leaders of other community-based, public, and private organizations that had contact with the faith-based organization being studied (Orr, 2000, p. 14).

To collect information at the county level, research assistants conducted in-person and telephone interviews. These interviews were semi-structured, using interview guides, and there was flexibility in terms of reading the questions exactly as printed. Focus groups were used with leaders of faith-based organizations who had provided leadership in offering large-scale programs at the county level. Moderators of these focus groups had a discussion guide but were nonetheless instructed to allow participants fairly free rein in discussing their experiences with welfare reform efforts (Orr, 2000).

As an example of the freedom of design choices that can occur in qualitative research projects, the study added to its data collection efforts interviews with state legislators, legislative staff, and California government agency workers, as well as participant observations of meetings and legislative hearings. The impetus for adding data collection to this level of government was because it was clear from the information gathered at the neighborhood and county levels that "the implementation of Charitable Choice was being delayed by the actions of state officials" (Orr, 2000, p. 15).

Results and Conclusions

At the risk of eliminating the most interesting or important aspects of this evaluation, we will focus on the research results of only the last two of the major questions asked by the evaluators: "What disincentives affect the willingness of faith-based programs to compete for welfare-to-work contracts?" and "What factors expand the capacity of faith-based organizations to participate in welfare-to-work programs?" The answers to these questions were derived from focus groups respondents in seven California counties and interviews with knowledgeable individuals over the two-year period of research.

Disincentives that were noted in the report are divided into three categories. In the first, *organizational capacity disincentives*, there were problems noted in obtaining and running contracts. For example, respondents noted that it was difficult to find out about the possible contracts that county governments were offering, as there was no central or easily accessible way to locate requests for proposals and to determine which agencies currently had contracts. The language of the requests for proposals was considered bureaucratic and difficult to understand, especially for people new to the idea of contracting with the government to provide services.

The second category of disincentives noted in the report related to *running the contract* should one be awarded to the faith-based organization. Issues noted here included the inability of these organizations to continue operating if payments from the county were delayed; the difficulty for organizations to modify and upgrade their facilities to meet government-mandated requirements, such as to provide day care services; and the "overhead" expenses of record-keeping, accounting, and program evaluation. Performance-based payments from government were seen as too risky to take on, particularly if county agencies did not provide sufficient referrals to the organization to enable them to fulfill the terms of the contract.

The third category of disincentives was not practical concerns, as were the first two, but rather *philosophical or ideological concerns* with the idea of applying for government contracts under the welfare-to-work program aegis. Faith-based organizations are primarily interested in spiritual issues rather than issues of creating and running long-term social service programs. Some respondents stated that the concepts behind Charitable Choice blurred the separation of church and state, and was part of a political payback by the Republican Party to conservative Christian congregations for their support of Republican candidates. The most ideologically liberal opponents of becoming involved with the welfare-to-work contracting process saw TANF as a cruel way to treat the poor and did not want to be associated with the program. Other opponents, liberal and conservative, did not want to lose their position as "prophetic" organizations, standing outside the governmental sphere and being able to criticize government leaders and programs. Government regulations also put important restrictions on the ability of faith-based organizations to evangelize to the recipients of services.

Six factors were associated with expanding the capacity of faith-based organizations to participate in the Charitable Choice welfare-to-work programs. The first was *knowledge* about the program. Liberal organizations wanted to be assured that the program was constitutional at both the national and state levels, while conservative organizations appreciated knowing that the provisions were written and sponsored by Senator Ashcroft, a conservative Pentecostal church member.

The second factor was *leadership by elected officials and their staff members*. Doing things such as increasing access to requests for proposals, making language in the requests for proposals simpler, holding bidders' conferences, and, particularly, interacting with faith-based organizations' leaders, "generated tangible results, especially among conservative evangelical and Pentecostal congregations" (Orr, 2000, p. 57). *Leadership from religious leaders and denominations* was the third factor. When theological and political reasons to participate were communicated, organizations (particularly evangelical faith-based ones), were more likely to compete for county contracts.

Factor four was *entrepreneurial leadership by religious leaders*. These leaders found ways around the barriers noted above in order to partner with other organizations and to provide services to TANF recipients. One place that these entrepreneurial leaders turned to is called a "*brokering institution*," the presence of which was factor five. Such an institution provides help for entrepreneurs in finding "appropriate partners, funding sources, and the technical expertise they need in realizing their visions" (Orr, 2000, p. 58).

The sixth factor was the presence of *intermediary institutions*. An intermediary institution is a nonprofit that is expressly created to assist faith-based organizations to apply for and run Charitable Choice social services, or a nonprofit that is already in existence that is currently providing services. By working with other organizations and creating coalitions and collaborations for service provision, faith-based organizations can be much better prepared to provide services, and the services provided will most likely be of more value to clients than if organizations try to move forward on their own.

Analyzing the Study

This section looks at the research study just described in terms of representativeness, extrapolation, trustworthiness, objectivity/confirmability, and interpretation, just like we did for the first example. We will look at each characteristic in turn.

Representativeness

One of the first questions we ask of any research is how representative are the results of the entire population that could have been involved as information sources. In this study, there are several "sub-studies" with different sources of information. The first level looks at faith-based organizations in neighborhoods. The researchers chose five neighborhoods (four in Los Angeles' central city and one in a suburban area nearby).

> The four urban neighborhoods were selected because, together, they roughly mirrored Los Angeles County's ethnic/racial diversity and because census data had suggested that these neighborhoods probably contain large numbers of welfare-to-work participants. The suburban neighborhood was selected because of its middle and upper middle class character and because of its geographical proximity to Old Long Beach's low-income neighborhoods (Orr, 2000, p. 13).

Though the authors note that the neighborhoods chosen "mirror" the county's diversity, for a study that is ostensibly about welfare reform in California, this appears biased since Los Angeles County cannot be considered representative of the entire state. The selection would have been appropriate had the study focused solely on welfare reform in Los Angeles County.

Interviews were conducted by the research team with "clergy and lay leaders from fifty faith-based organizations" (Orr, 2000, p. 14). There is no mention of how many organizations there were in these neighborhoods, how these fifty organizations were chosen, or how many leaders were actually interviewed (there may have been only one leader from each organization, or more than one—the report is not clear). Leaders from other organizations that interacted with faith-based organizations also were interviewed, although it is not clear how many such interviews there were or how they were chosen. In sum, the representativeness of the neighborhood-level information is clearly not high, even for Los Angeles County.

Eight counties were chosen to represent all counties in California in terms of the interactions between government agencies and faith-based organizations. They were selected as "representatives of the state's diverse economies and cultures" (Orr, 2000, p. 15). Counties in Southern California "dominated" the sample because "over half of the state's population of welfare-to-work participants" live in that part of the state (Orr, p. 15). The exact selection process is not given, nor are any figures provided to show on what variables the counties were representative of the state. Later in the process, focus groups were created in six of these eight counties (selection process unknown). The people invited to be in the focus groups were selected based on "their demonstrated leadership in offering major county-related welfare-to-work programs" (Orr, p. 15). Focus groups are not necessarily supposed to be representative in the same way a random sample is; rather they should be composed of people who can provide insight into the research question at hand. Still, it is not clear how this particular group of respondents is insightful on the question. No numbers are provided, either of the entire population or of those in the focus groups.

The final set of interviews took place with "four legislative staff members, a California state senator, three staff members in the California Department of Social Services, and two staff members in the Employment Development Department" (Orr, 2000, p. 16). The degree of representativeness of this collection of individuals can only be guessed at.

We noted earlier in this chapter that most qualitative evaluators do not have a list of the entire population from which to randomly select respondents. In fact, one of the first steps in this research project was to conduct a census of faith-based organizations in the chosen neighborhoods and counties. Nonetheless, concerning representativeness, there was considerable lack of clarity in the selection of the respondents for this study. Convenience in finding and obtaining permission to interview the respondents seems to have been the major approach used. Also, no mention was made of theoretical sampling in search of redundancy and saturation.

Extrapolation
The degree of extrapolation possible in this study is similar to the degree or representativeness in it: we do not really know if it is or is not transferable. Given the number of interviews and the amount of work that went into the study, we may find ourselves believing that it *must be*

similar to what is happening throughout the state of California, and that results from California can usefully inform us about results in the rest of the nation as well. There are no blanket statements regarding extrapolation in the report, although there are comments that would lead a reader to believe that the author believes that the results can be applied to all of the state of California. Without further information, however, these assertions are not supported by much evidence.

Applying the ideas that Schofield (1990) presents that were discussed above, we can see that Orr (2000) indicates that the evaluation studied the typical situations (at least in Los Angeles County), used multiple sites for gathering data (again, this is done most thoroughly in Los Angeles County), studied institutions on the leading edge of change (the changing role of faith-based organizations) and also selected a site (California) that is often thought to be on the forefront of what the other states will eventually do as well. It thus seems that Orr's work could be quite transferable. The write-up, however, downplays the transferability of the data and analysis, preferring to keep the context very much tied to California. The degree of extrapolation is probably greatest for Los Angeles County, because of the number of neighborhoods examined there, but is low when thinking about transferring to the entire state.

Trustworthiness through Triangulation and Transparency

Trustworthiness is often a difficult characteristic to demonstrate with a qualitative study. The author of the report does not describe the methodological steps taken to increase trustworthiness through triangulation of analysts, such as having more than one person code the transcripts of interviews. It is also not clear if a draft of the report was provided to the respondents to check for their insights and their agreement that these are the important themes that occurred to them. What we seem to have is a single-authored analysis and reporting of the analysis. In terms of transparency, in this case, there is a team of researchers conducting the interviews and focus groups. Presumably, all are adequately trained and capable, although no information is provided on the topic.

Objectivity/Confirmability

The author of this study (Orr, 2000) does not explicitly discuss issues of objectivity or confirmability. Instead, we are left to imagine that the picture painted in the report is correct. The designer of this research used a variety of information sources, engaging in the use of multiple sources of data (a type of triangulation), which, if they agreed, provided the essence of confirmability: independent sources of information that agreed about what happened. It is not clear from the write-up, however, that triangulation worked as intended, as it is sometimes unclear as to whether there were separate measures set up to capture the same sorts of information.

Interpretation

The interpretation of these results follows the four interpretive moments described by Yanow (2006b). The first interpretive moment is when the persons who turn out to be the sources of information for the evaluation actually experience something. One example is when religious leaders experienced the inability to access the Requests for Proposals. This experience was then interpreted by the leaders, probably in different ways. The second time of interpretation was when a member of the research team talked to the religious leaders. Both the religious leader and the research team member were interpreting the situation at this point. The third interpretive moment was when Orr wrote the report. A great deal of internal and intuitive analysis took place as he did so. The final interpretive moment is when readers take a look at the report. (There is also a fifth and sixth moment: when the reader reads the report, in this case, secondhand, filtered through my interpretation.)

A few of the conclusions noted in the report are clearly the result of interpreting information gathered and might be interpreted differently by other researchers, necessitating triangulation of analysts. For example:

- "There are good grounds for Congress's positive assumptions concerning the ability of religious groups to play the social service roles envisioned by the 1996 Personal Responsibility and Work Opportunity Reconciliation Act" (Orr, 2000, p. 61).
- "The capacity to conduct social service programs is different from the capacity to expand and to diversify these program offerings. When nonprofits expand and diversify their program offerings, for example, they usually need more complex organizational structures and expanded staffs" (Orr, 2000, p. 62).

- "The state's faith-based organizations, under certain conditions, can indeed expand their contributions to welfare reform. Faith-based organizations have the capacity to offer a range of publicly-supported services. But, in most cases, they cannot function as comprehensive welfare agencies. Most should not even try. They can do many things well, and they will best serve welfare-to-work participants when the limits to their capacity are acknowledged and respected" (Orr, 2000, p. 64).

Because of the problems noted earlier regarding representativeness, extrapolation, trustworthiness, and objectivity/confirmability, we may have doubts about the interpretations of the data presented in the final section of the report. While it is easy enough to ask questions about some of the methodological aspects of the report ("How many interviews were conducted?" "How many possible interview subjects were there?" and so on), it is somewhat more difficult to step back to think of questions regarding the interpretation of data, such as, "Why do you believe that religious groups are able to do what was called for in the PRWORA of 1996?" or "What are the reasons behind your understanding that faith-based organizations can play an important role in moving people from welfare to work?" These judgments are interpretations of the data but are not fully justified within this report. An evaluator who looked at the same data, but had a philosophical or ideological opposition to the Charitable Choice policy provisions, might read the data very differently.

CONCLUSION

This chapter has examined qualitative research and evaluation. Five key aspects of qualitative methods have been explored: representativeness, extrapolation, trustworthiness, objectivity/confirmability, and interpretation. We have also looked at two examples of qualitative evaluations of facets of the welfare reform law, analyzing them in terms of these five aspects to see how things play out in "the real world" of policy and program evaluation. The next chapter provides similar information on the topic of quantitative methods in evaluation.

6

Using Quantitative Approaches to Understand What the Policy Did

Continuing with Part II, this chapter devotes itself to describing and then applying quantitative methods to evaluate policy outcomes. Quantitative methods are the hallmark of the so-called hard sciences of physics, biology, chemistry, and so on. Things exist, they can be measured (more or less) precisely, and the relationships between them can be specified with some degree of accuracy or probability. This is the essence of the quantitative approach to science. While it is safe to say that qualitative methods are probably older, it is also safe to say that during most of the twentieth century, even social scientists for the most part wanted to become better versed in quantitative methods, particularly the use of more and more advanced statistical techniques. As the previous chapter shows, the contentious relationships of previous years between qualitative and quantitative researchers and evaluators has been calmed by the realization that qualitative methods have an important place in the toolkit of evaluators and researchers, just as quantitative methods do.

This chapter provides an overview of quantitative methods, particularly from an evaluation perspective. We then use two examples of evaluations of aspects of the welfare reform law to apply our understanding of the strengths and limitations of this style of analysis.

DESCRIPTION OF THE QUANTITATIVE APPROACH TO SOCIAL POLICY EVALUATION

Quantitative methods–using researchers or evaluators bring with them the underlying belief that there is a reality beyond any one individual's senses that exists independently of the perception of it. Some of the philosophical debate concerning positivists and constructionists has already been discussed and need not be repeated here. Still, it is important to understand what one is getting in for when using quantitative methods.

SPECIFIC QUANTITATIVE RESEARCH METHODS IN SOCIAL POLICY EVALUATION

This section describing quantitative research and evaluation methods is necessarily brief. Still, as in the previous chapter on qualitative methods, it is necessary to present the material here so that these concepts can be applied in the last part of the chapter. We discuss several aspects of quantitative methods, including secondary data analysis, survey research, standardized measures, design issues, and inferential statistical analysis. There is some overlap between this material and the material relating to rational policy analysis techniques covered in Chapter 4, but the intent here is different, and repetition has been kept to a minimum.

Secondary data analysis

One of the more common approaches to policy evaluation among quantitative researchers is the use of secondary data. Secondary data are data that were collected by someone else, for other purposes. As Dudley (2010) notes, "A good question to begin with is to ask whether *new* data are needed" (p. 134, emphasis in original). If data are already available, it is a great savings of time and money to use them. The data used are often collected from surveys (see next section) but this is not necessarily the case.

Depositories of secondary data sets (many of them quite useful in examining social policy–related questions) exist throughout the world, and the data sets are often available without charge. A general caution regarding the use of secondary data is to choose data sets that have information that is pertinent to particular evaluation questions, rather than to find interesting what is already available. One should always start with the research questions to be answered and then search for the data that are already accessible.

Despite the relative ease of identifying and accessing previously gathered information, the use of secondary data can be filled with unanticipated problems, so a researcher should be careful regarding the details of the process. An excellent introduction to the process is available from The University of Wisconsin's Data and Information Services Center (DISC) (2003, http://www.disc.wisc.edu/types/secondary.htm). While some of the information is specific to the University of Wisconsin's context, most of the website is generalizable to the use of any secondary data set. Here is a list of some of the tasks to undertake, once an appropriate data set has been found and a codebook has been secured.

The basics pieces of information that you will need and tasks you must perform are:

- The data structure—rectangular, hierarchical, etc.
- The variables that you are interested in, including their column location(s), variable type (alpha or numeric); additional formatting information (number of decimals, whether there are blanks in the field).
- Identify essential supplemental variables such as unique case identifiers, weights, and the like that are necessary for using the data correctly.
- Prepare labels to identify the variables and values on your output.
- You should also note some baseline marginals to test. For example, if the codebook lists the number of cases by geographic area, you might want to consider comparing your extraction results to this table (DISC, 2003).

One of the best sources for secondary data sets is the Inter-University Consortium for Political and Social Research (ICPSR) (www.icpsr.umich. edu) which has thousands of data sets that one can download. At the time this chapter was written, a total of 58 data sets relating to the keywords "welfare reform" were available, including the data set for the Three City Study, which is one of the examples at the end of this chapter.

Survey research

Survey research is one of the most popular forms of quantitative data collection, at least partially because it is relatively easy to conduct. However, to collect meaningful data that are useful in evaluating a policy or program, great care must be used. Some of the issues of concern with survey research include sampling, question development, and survey construction.

Sampling

If the goal of the survey is to gather information from the portion of the population that *could* be surveyed in order to generalize their responses to the entire population, then the researcher must be very concerned with the representativeness of the sample. Representative sampling is based on the assumption that the researcher has a list of all the possible respondents. While this is not always the case, and methods have been developed to handle situations where there is no list, the closer to reality the assumption is, the more easily a representative sampling process can be obtained.

Two families of sampling exist, probability sampling and non-probability sampling. The ones that are best suited for generalizing to a broader population from the sample are random sampling, systematic random sampling, stratified random sampling, and cluster sampling (Dudley, 2010, p. 150). The key aspect of each of these four approaches to sampling is that a random process is used to select who is chosen to be surveyed and who is not. It is the random selection of participants that leads to considerable faith in the representativeness of the sample. A relatively small number of respondents can be representative of a very large population if the sample is drawn correctly—for example, it only takes 384 people out of a population of 1,000,000 to have a margin of error of five percent (Dudley, p. 159).

Non-probability sampling is a process of choosing respondents who have a very small chance of being representative of the entire population. The main non-probability sampling techniques include convenience sampling, snowball sampling, quota sampling, and purposive sampling. Such techniques have limited usefulness for evaluation but can sometimes be appropriate.

Convenience sampling uses easy-to-reach subjects, such as students in an instructor's classroom or welfare applicants in a waiting room at the particular time that an evaluator has time to conduct interviews. It can be useful to get a quick idea of the types of responses one might receive and can be good for pre-testing questions and topics before a more representative sample is chosen. Snowball sampling consists of starting with one respondent who is appropriate and having him or her introduce the researcher to other potential respondents who are similar. This technique is particularly useful when approaching difficult-to-find respondents (such as the homeless or youthful runaways) or elites who may be slow to trust an evaluator or researcher.

Quota sampling requires predetermining the types and number of people who are to be surveyed. The design may call for 100 total respondents, with 75 females and 25 males, for example. Once any particular group of respondents has reached its assigned number, the surveyors no longer collect information from any more people in that category. While this sounds as if one can call this representative (assuming that the percentages in the quotas are similar to the prevalence of such people in the population) it often happens that quota sampling masks a convenience sampling approach. This occurs because of the way each quota is filled—usually with the first people matching the desired demographics.

The final non-probability approach is purposive sampling, also known as "judgmental sampling." In this technique, the evaluator chooses who the respondents are based on knowledge of the respondents. Often, the basis for selection is being atypical in some way—being more successful, or less successful, than others in a program, for example. In this way, specific correlates of success can be discovered, or the range of barriers to achievement of desired outcomes can be explored. In either case, the information is specifically designed to be unrepresentative of the larger population.

Question development

Questions for the survey must be developed to elicit the information desired. Possible types of information (Dudley, 2010, p. 175, following Patton, 1987) and an example of each type are:

- *Experience or behaviors*: How many hours did you work this past week for pay?
- *Opinions or beliefs*: What do you think keeps you from working more hours?

- *Feelings:* How do you feel about the way TANF program staff treat you?
- *Knowledge:* What are some of the forms you need to file every six months?
- *Sensory:* What do you recall seeing and hearing when you went to the TANF offices the last time you visited there?
- *Demographic:* How many years of schooling have you completed?

The purpose of asking any question is to collect information that will be useful in answering a research or an evaluation question. Questions can be *closed-ended* (that is, respondents choose a response from a list provided to them) or *open-ended* (respondents provide their response based on what they want to say or write). Closed-ended questions are easier to handle in terms of data entry and analysis. Open-ended responses give a more complete understanding of the respondent's views. They may need to be coded in qualitative ways or reduced to a list of close-ended responses.

The closed-ended question designer must consider the format of the responses as well. Will respondents receive a list of possible answers, similar to a multiple-choice test? Will respondents have a scale to place a mark on to show the extent of their agreement, for example from "completely satisfied" to "not at all satisfied"? Other approaches exist as well, and the question developer should be familiar with them all.

One common problem in posing useful questions is that their meaning could be unclear due to the use of an ambiguous term or phrase. "Has the program been good?" might be too vague to provide actionable information. Another problem is the "double-barreled" question; a question that is two questions in one with possibly different answers— for example, the question "Does your case worker treat you respectfully and in a friendly way?" may be true in terms of "respect," but untrue when looking at "friendliness." A third problem is that the question may be leading, or may provide respondents with a clue as to how they should answer, such as, "In what ways does being employed make you a better parent?" (Dudley, 2010, p. 175). Additional problems can be identified, so it is important to work with the idea that developing useful questions that relate to a particular evaluation question may take considerable time to create. Pretesting questions with people similar to the people who will answer the questions is imperative.

Methodologically, poorly worded questions introduce what is essentially random error into the answers the survey receives. People are not really sure how to answer the question, so they pick an answer almost randomly. Error in the responses will decrease the ability to find meaningful results, leading to wasted time, lost effort, and poorly used funds.

Survey construction

The construction of the survey instrument goes beyond choosing useful questions. It also encompasses the overall length of the instrument, the appearance of the document, and the order of the questions. The length of the survey is related to the information needed to answer the research questions. But the survey also has to gain and retain the interest of respondents, so it is important to make it attractive and easy to fill in (whether the respondent or an interviewer is filling in the form). The order of the questions matters as well. Generally, non-sensitive, easy to answer, and basic information questions are placed at the beginning of a survey, while sensitive questions, or questions that require more in-depth thinking, are placed near the end. This is because respondents may want to break off the survey when sensitive or difficult questions are posed. If they do so, most of the information that is desired from the respondent has already been collected and not as much is lost by having the interviewee leave before completing the questions.

Another consideration in the ordering of questions is to cluster questions about a similar subject matter. Having questions about the same topic in close proximity to each other helps both the interviewee and interviewer focus on one thing at a time, and increases the quality of the information collected (Dudley, 2010). Questions that are more general should come before questions that are more specific, in order not to interfere with client answers. As an example, when interviewing a TANF client concerning possible barriers to obtaining work, the order might be like this:

Using the scale below, to what extent do you believe that conditions beyond your control keep you from working as much as you would like?

Not at all   Some   A great deal
  1   2   3   4   5   6   7   8   9   10

Being more specific, how much do the following get in the way of your working as much as you would like?

Lack of Transportation

Not at all				Some				A great deal	
1	2	3	4	5	6	7	8	9	10

Lack of Child Care

Not at all				Some				A great deal	
1	2	3	4	5	6	7	8	9	10

Additional potential barriers beyond lack of transportation and lack of child care could be found through a literature search and added to the survey.

Standardized measures

Standardized measures are frequently used in program evaluations to determine changes in recipients. A standardized measure is an instrument that has been previously tested in order to have known levels of reliability and validity with certain populations. Instruments exist to measure many different attitudes, beliefs, and other concepts. Sources of instruments include Fischer and Corcoran (2007) and the Mental Measurements Yearbook (Buros Institute of Mental Measurement, 2007). Standardized measures provide a sort of comparison group already built in—the norms of an instrument are usually reported, and as long as they are based on a population similar to what the program serves, a comparison is apt. Typically, however, the norms for the instrument are based on different populations, so it is wise to examine additional literature that reports results from other populations.

Design issues

One of the largest differences between qualitative and quantitative research methods relates to the design of the research. Much of the scientific rigor associated with quantitative methods is due to the design of the studies conducted. According to the canons of social science, as developed by Campbell and Stanley (1963), *experimental designs*, using randomly selected participants who are randomly assigned to a treatment or control group, are necessary to show conclusively that the treatment caused any observed changes in the outcomes of the participants, measured with appropriately rigorous instruments. There are several distinct designs that meet the criteria for experimental designs, such as the experimental post-test only, the experimental pre-test–post-test, and the Solomon 4-group designs. These designs accomplish their work in showing a causal link by eliminating other explanations, called "threats to internal validity." (Without going into detail here, some of the threats to such validity noted by methodologists are selection, history, instrumentation, regression to the mean, testing, maturation, and mortality.) Once the threats to internal validity have been controlled, the most logical explanation is that the treatment is responsible for the changes observed.

Another class of designs is called *quasi-experimental*. *Quasi*, the Latin word meaning "as if," indicates that these designs act "as if" they are experimental, although they are not. The primary reason they are not truly experimental is that they do not use random assignment of respondents to either a treatment or a control group. Instead, they use a comparison group, which may or may not be truly equivalent. The more similar the comparison group (which does not receive the treatment) and the treatment group are, the more the quasi-experimental design approximates the corresponding experimental design. It is sometimes debated whether a time series approach, which collects information over a longer period of time, is able to be its own comparison group (although the addition of another group as a comparison makes for a stronger design). There are many different quasi-experimental designs, each with its own problems in terms of which alternate explanations (threats to internal validity) it is strong at controlling and for which ones it is not strong. Best practice indicates that evaluators should analyze which threats to internal validity are strongest in a particular study and choose the design that is most able to control those particular threats.

An additional set of designs, called *non-experimental*, also exists. These designs have no random assignment and do not include a comparison group. They consist of one group made up of people who receive the intervention. Simple one group pre-test and post-test evaluations fall into this category, as do the post-test only and time series designs. These are not able to control many (if any) threats to internal validity, but with the use of advanced statistical controls, such evaluations may still provide useful, if not causal, information on the effects of a policy. Having multiple replications of research using non-experimental designs, when they come to similar conclusions, also provides assurance that a program can change clients. In such cases, the use of effect sizes can provide compelling information on program efficacy (Mindel & Hoefer, 2006).

INFERENTIAL STATISTICAL ANALYSIS

Because of the nature of program evaluation and policy analysis, it is fairly rare to use experimental designs, and most of the literature on welfare reform outcomes uses some form of quasi-experimental or non-experimental design. Readers can (correctly) dispute research results by attacking the design used. As a way to shore up results' validity, and also to use survey results in lieu of research using classical design strategies, advanced inferential statistical approaches to data analysis are frequently used.

Such approaches derive from an econometric view of the world and start with building a model of independent variables that have an impact on the dependent variable. Control variables (generally demographic variables such as gender, race or ethnicity, and age) are also frequently added to the model to show if differences associated with those variables exist. For example, Knab et al. (2009) create a model to explain "the effects of welfare and child support policies on the incidence of marriage following a nonmarital birth" using information collected about mothers unmarried at the time of the study's beginning. Their information is part of a large data set, called the "Fragile Families Study." The outcome measured by this model (the dependent variable) is whether the mother and father marry within five years of a child's birth. Independent variables examined were the level of welfare generosity and level of child-support enforcement. Control variables in the model were mother's age, mother's age at first birth, number of children, education level, race and ethnicity, relationship with the child's father (cohabiting or dating), mother depressed (yes or no), whether the child's father had children from previous relationships, and whether the father had been incarcerated in the previous year (Knab, et al.).

Multivariate approaches such as this can test for the level of impact from each independent and control variable, one at a time, "holding constant" the many other variables included in the model. The more variables included in the model, the more cases there must be in the data set to allow for sufficient variation in the variables. Knab et al. (2009) wrote in the conclusions section of their study that: "We find support for the hypotheses that welfare generosity (i.e., higher cash benefits and more lenient sanctions) and strong support enforcement are associated with lower rates of marriage. But we also find support for the alternative" (Knab, et al, 2009, p. 304).

Unfortunately for people who wish for a clear answer, this type of conclusion is common. As frustrating as this sort of conclusion is to such a reader, it is also (or even more) frustrating to the researchers who hope to influence policy. To policy-makers, however, this sort of result presents a good-news/bad-news scenario. The good news is that, simplified enough (as most political use of social science research is), the results can be used to support whichever side of the debate the policy-maker is on. The bad news is that it can be used the same way by their political opponents!

ADVANTAGES OF THE QUANTITATIVE APPROACH TO SOCIAL POLICY EVALUATION

Once data are gathered, a number of useful procedures can be carried out. First, the evaluator may describe the respondents and the information collected about them and their situations, behaviors, ideas, beliefs, and attitudes. The most basic level of description is to use frequency counts: the number of respondents; their gender, race, or ethnicity, and so on. Description also includes both measures of central tendency and of dispersion. It is helpful to know what the mean number of months of TANF receipt is, for example, or the median age of children enrolled in the program. Dispersion around the central point helps us understand the range of responses. For example, if we are comparing two groups of TANF recipients (non-randomly assigned), one group of which is to receive extra training while the other group is not, before we begin we want to determine if the two groups are fairly comparable. One bit of data to ascertain comparability is to know the average length of time each group has already been receiving TANF. It may be that the averages for the two groups are very similar, but that the dispersion around the mean is quite different. Perhaps, at baseline, in the group to receive treatment, most respondents are near the average, while in the second group, some respondents have been receiving benefits for only a short time, while still others have been on the program on for a relatively long time. These groups would not really be comparable, and any comparisons made would be suspect. A number of ways to measure dispersion exist, and the most apt one will vary from situation to situation, depending primarily on the level of measurement of the variable (nominal, ordinal, interval, or ratio).

This example points out another considerable advantage of quantitative evaluation methods: it is possible to make comparisons quickly and meaningfully. At its heart, outcome evaluation is a comparison process. A typical question for an evaluation is: What were the effects of the program on the participants compared to "something else"? The "something else" can be "doing nothing," providing "treatment as usual," or giving "some other alternative intervention" that might claim to be as good as the new treatment, or may include additional or fewer program components.

Beyond the important numerical descriptions of respondents, quantitative methods allow for the use of much more advanced statistical techniques, ones that can show relationships between variables, using multivariate analysis, as mentioned earlier. The beauty of using quantitative methods to note and expand on the connections between concepts is that the process can be replicated. Unlike qualitative methods, quantitative methods have structured ways to show representativeness, external generalizability, reliability, and validity (what is termed by qualitative methodologists *objectivity/confirmability*). These are significant and important advantages. The importance of these traits is in their ability to improve the interpretation of the information collected. Interpretation of data, just as in qualitative research, is the ultimate goal of research or evaluation. (Of course, as noted in Chapter 5, qualitative methods have their own strengths and advantages.)

CRITIQUES OF THE QUANTITATIVE APPROACH TO SOCIAL POLICY EVALUATION

Critics of quantitative methods are not silent in the face of the arguments in favor of these methods. The first level of critique is philosophical: the quantitative approach is heavily dependent on the idea of an external reality waiting to be measured, described, and analyzed. If one takes issue with this position, the rest of the debate is meaningless. Assuming, for the sake of debate, that there are elements of an external world that exist independently of the perceiver, a criticism of quantitative methods is that they are inherently reductionist, in that they take complex phenomena and simplify them to the point of uselessness. Quantitative models, no matter how many cases are included and how many variables are measured, can never be wholly accurate. The interpretation of data, limited to numerical points on a scale and possibly devoid of much of the meaning of the data to the respondent, cannot be assumed to be correctly applicable to the world outside the evaluator's door. Most quantitative output interpretation must be probabilistic because the analytical procedures are designed to show, for example, the probability that two numerical variables are correlated beyond "a reasonable doubt" of .05. A critic may ask how certain one's interpretation can be, for example, if one is willing to be wrong five times out of 100 (and that is assuming that all the other aspects of design measurement, validity, and reliability were handled perfectly)?

In addition, quantitative research is faulted for being inflexible compared to qualitative methods (Berg, 2009). Designs, measures, sampling, and statistical procedures are laid out before the research begins and are not to be changed unless harm to the subjects is occurring. Such inflexibility in the face of incoming information can be a problem and might block researchers from discovering important results.

Finally, because of the need for advanced training to properly use statistical procedures, the quantitative evaluator tends to come across as the "expert-who-cannot-be-challenged"—this effect is difficult to overcome, no matter how much the evaluator tries. There are only so many people in the world who know (or want to know) how to use structural equation modeling in their day-to-day lives, and it is safe to say that the world of low-income persons is probably not awash with such individuals, any more than is the world in general. Thus the likelihood of including client perspectives in the direct analysis of results is small and problematic.

USING QUANTITATIVE METHODS IN RESEARCHING TANF OUTCOMES

In the previous chapter on qualitative methods, two examples were provided at the end, in which the principles in the chapter were applied to published studies. This chapter does this as well, pointing out both strengths and weaknesses in the studies chosen. The two research efforts included in this chapter are purposefully selected to show some of the options available to scholars as they create their research plans and conduct their analyses. Each example will be discussed in terms of its background and research objectives, the methods used, and its results and conclusions. It will also be analyzed to determine how well the research solved possible problems of quantitative methods, such as sampling, measures, design, analysis, and interpretation.

Example 1:

B. Frogner, R. Moffitt, and D. Ribar (2009). How families are doing nine years after welfare reform: 2005 evidence from the Three-City Study. In J. Ziliak (Ed.), *Welfare Reform and Its Long Term Consequences for America's Poor* (pp. 140–171), New York: Cambridge University Press.

Background and Research Objectives
This study addresses issues relating to the economic outcomes of welfare reform. (Note: the data set used in this study is available for free download from the Inter-University Consortium for Political and Social Research at www.icpsr.umich.edu.) There are three questions that fall under this general topic that are addressed. First, "How have patterns of welfare use among families changed between 1999 and 2005, when the latest data were collected?" Second, "What are the economic, demographic, social, and health correlates of different types of transition outcomes?" Finally, "What role does work play in helping families become economically self-reliant after leaving welfare?" (Frogner et al., 2009, pp. 141–142).

Methods used
The data used in this manuscript are from the "Three-City Study," which is a set of responses collected in three waves from 1999 to 2005 in the cities of Boston, San Antonio, and Chicago. These cities were chosen "because they were representative of large urban areas in the United

States and because they were in states with markedly different welfare policies" (Frogner et al., 2009, p. 143). Advantages of this data set compared to other data sets that have been used to address the same questions are that it is one of the longest-running panel studies of low-income families; the latest wave of data collection was recent (as of the time the paper was written), including information on the recession of the early 2000s; and, perhaps most important, it contains information on low-income families that were TANF recipients at the start of the study and also families that were not TANF recipients at that time. Thus it is possible to compare the situation early in the implementation of welfare reform and how the families were doing seven years later for the two different groups. Frogner et al. state that "the survey is rich in information and detail on respondent well-being and behavior at each of the three interview waves, having collected a comprehensive set of household income components for all household members" (p. 141).

After excluding information relating to some families for age, lack of children in the home, and other reasons, a total of 1,555 caregivers were included. These respondents are similar to all respondents, and whatever few differences exist that can be attributed to attrition bias are controlled for statistically (Frogner et al., 2009, p. 143).

Results and conclusions
The results of this study are used to address the three study questions. The answers are nuanced and have a lot of "it depends" quality to them. Restating the research question and then describing the results linked to that particular question will assist us in keeping everything straight.

How have patterns of welfare use among families changed? The simple result is that welfare use declined, from nearly one-third of the respondents of the Three-City Study in 1999 to about one-ninth in 2005.

What are the economic, demographic, social, and health correlates of different types of transition outcomes? The results indicate that the caregivers who remained on TANF for all three waves of data collection:

> . . . worked less, had lower rates of marriage, and reported worse health and higher rates of disability than other caregivers. On or off welfare, many caregivers in our sample remained needy. By the third wave of the

study, two-thirds were receiving Medicaid and just under half were receiving food stamps (Frogner et al., 2009, p. 167).

Caregivers who remained off of TANF for all three waves had "the highest incomes and the best economic circumstances" (Frogner, p. 168). The other groups (those who stayed on welfare continuously, left welfare by either wave 2 or wave 3, or entered TANF on either wave 2 or wave 3) showed little difference in income among themselves. What seems to make the most difference in increasing income for TANF leavers and those who never received TANF are obtaining employment and marrying or entering a cohabiting relationship. For continuous recipients, marrying or cohabiting did not have a significant effect on income.

What role does work play in helping families become economically self-reliant after leaving welfare? The data indicate "positive" effects after nine years of welfare reform for most families at the time of the data collection in 2005. "On average, the caregivers in our sample were enjoying higher incomes and lower rates of poverty in 2005 than they did in 1999, with the economic gains coming primarily from increased earnings" (Frogner, 2009, p. 169). The picture the data paint is not entirely bright, however, as almost half of the families remained poor and many families depended on other government programs such as Supplemental Security Income (SSI), Social Security Disability Income (SSDI), and food stamps. People who left TANF but who were not connected to employment (so-called "disconnected leavers") were the worst off.

The authors provide two key policy recommendations: maintain in-kind benefit programs and do something about people not on TANF who are not employed or employable.

Analyzing the Study
How well does this study meet the criteria for a "good" evaluation or policy assessment? We will examine it in five areas: sampling, measures, design, analysis, and interpretation.

Sampling
The key issue when discussing sampling is representativeness. The authors point out in their write-up that one of the concerns in their work

is that it includes only three cities in its sampling frame. Despite the efforts to say that Boston, Chicago, and San Antonio are representative of large urban areas, no information is presented to bolster that argument. The three states involved, Massachusetts, Illinois, and Texas, were chosen because they were very different from each other and might illuminate different patterns of results. This "maximum difference" approach is interesting, but the paper does not make comparisons between the cities, so this does not help with making a strong case for external generalizability. No information is presented in this paper regarding the process of sampling within the three chosen cities, so we do not know how representative the findings are at the city level either. Some comparisons are made to the results of other studies, which lends support to the data's being at least somewhat representative of the population of low-income or vulnerable families across the country.

Measures

The authors provide some detail on the measures used for each of their concepts. Most of the variables are easily understood control variables; race/ethnicity (Hispanic, non-Hispanic black; and non-Hispanic white); education (no high school degree, high school degree/GED, above high school/GED); age; living arrangements (married, cohabiting, single); and number of people in the household. How other control variables were measured is less obvious: self-reported health status, level of functional disability, whether depressed or not, having experienced domestic violence, and level of network support are variables whose measure is not discussed in this report. Program participation rate and employment measures are unclear, as well.

The measurement of the variable of income is discussed extensively. Income is measured at the individual level and then aggregated to the household. Many sources of income are asked about: income from the earned income tax credit (EITC); TANF income; monthly earnings of others living in the household; food stamps, SSI program income, SSDI income of the individual and others in the household, income from other Social Security programs, and "other" income. This variable seems the most carefully delineated in this write-up.

Because this was a multi-year project and the data set is available from depositories, it is likely that all of the variables are fully and explicitly defined elsewhere, and in other publications from this project.

Still, for someone who is reading only this particular write-up, questions about measurement are many.

Design
The design used, time-series with statistical controls, is very common in quantitative welfare-reform-policy assessments. With only three data points, it is certainly a short time series, and one might wish for more recent data than 2005 given that the copyright date on the chapter is 2009. Still, it is better than a cross-sectional (or one-point data collection) design. It is heartening to know that there was relatively little respondent mortality across the three waves of data collection.

Analysis
The statistical techniques used by Frogner et al. (2009) included frequency counts, means, percentages, logit estimates, and ordinary least squares (OLS) regression analysis. Given the questions that were asked of the data, their use was appropriate. Without knowing all the details of the data, it is possible that additional modeling techniques could have been employed. However, there did not seem to be any errors in choice of statistical procedures or analysis of the data.

Interpretation
As with many quantitative papers, the foundations of the manuscript receive many more pages than does the discussion of the results. When set up in typical academic fashion, the groundwork pieces of literature review, methods (including design and measures), and statistical output take up the bulk of the paper. This is because the believability of the interpretation rests almost entirely on these issues. If the design or measures are ambiguous or flawed in some way, then the analysis is a case of "garbage in–garbage out." With the ease of creating output that fits into long tables, it can sometimes be a challenge to find what the authors believe is their contribution to the literature or the policy implications of their work.

The manuscript does not suffer overmuch from this condition. The multiple ways of analyzing the data across the different groups of respondents (respondents who stay on TANF, those who were never on, those who get on, and those who get off), with different independent variables, all make for a great deal of detail and varying results to explain. While readers may wish for a simple answer to the questions posed, providing simple answers to complex data outcomes is ultimately not accurate and may provide a falsely clear picture of the results. Two pages (168–169) provide the clearest short explication of the results, and even these pages are filled with "on one hand, but on the other hand" statements. An example of this relates to the question of whether work pays; that is, whether work provides more income than the loss of benefits takes away. Work does pay, the authors state,

> for employed leavers. However, it does not do so overall; when leavers as a whole are considered, employed and nonemployed combined, increases in average own earnings are completely offset by declines in TANF and Food Stamp benefits. Incomes for leavers rise, on average, but this is because of increases in other household members' earnings and increases in disability payments. But, on average, going off welfare does not result in sufficient work to compensate for the loss of benefits (Frogner et al., 2009, p. 169).

The lack of definitiveness in discussing the results should not be taken as a criticism of the authors or their study—it is merely a fact of life and a result of the ability of quantitative researchers to delve into the large-scale data sets with a variety of questions to ask and tools with which to provide answers.

Example 2:

D. Bloom, S. Scrivener, C. Michalopoulos, P. Morris, R. Hendra, D. Adams-Ciardullo, J. Walter, with W. Vargas (2002): Jobs First: Final Report on Connecticut's Welfare Reform Initiative, New York: Manpower Demonstration Research Corporation.

Background and Research Objectives

This example was chosen for several reasons. First, it is an experimental design, showing the ability of welfare reform programs to conduct very high-level research to examine the impact of state methods of implementing welfare reform legislation on clients. Second, it is 285 pages long and an extremely detailed write-up of the entire evaluation project, provided under contract from the State of Connecticut, conducted by a prestigious research firm, and paid for by the United States Department of Health and Human Services, the Ford Foundation, the Smith Richardson Foundation, and others. Thus, unlike the previous example, which presented only a portion of the entire project, this example should have everything a quantitative research project can have. (It is possible to download the full final report from the Manpower Demonstration Research Corporation's Web site, http://www.mdrc.org/publications/90/overview.html.)

The Connecticut version of welfare reform was titled "Jobs First," and it was unique in many ways. "Jobs First has attracted national attention because it includes all the features that are central to most states' current welfare programs, it has one of the shortest time limits in the nation, and it is one of the few programs of its kind that has been subject to a rigorous evaluation, including an assessment of effects on participants' children" (Bloom et al., 2002, p. ES-1). The research objectives or questions of the Jobs First evaluation were to detail the implementation of the law, particularly in terms of the services, mandates, and messages of the new program, on one hand, and the time limit, on the other. The evaluation also was designed to study the effects of Jobs First compared to the AFDC program (which was allowed to continue in parallel in order to conduct the evaluation) on the variables of employment and public assistance, non-economic outcomes such as job characteristics, material hardship and health care coverage, effects on children in the affected families, and the benefits and costs ratio of the program (Bloom et al. 2002, p. Sum-15).

Methods used

This evaluation was ambitious and covered not only the implementation of the Jobs First program in terms of services, mandates, messages, and time limits on client receipt of services, but also an evaluation of client outcomes. In order to attribute any changes in client outcomes to the differences between Jobs First (the new program, which had clients be subject to welfare reform policies) and AFDC (the old program, which had clients be subject to prior welfare rules), evaluators used an experimental design where clients were randomly assigned to either the new or the old program. Between January of 1996 and February of 1997, about 4,800 applicants for welfare and recipients received a random assignment to one program or the other. (This experiment was begun before the PRWORA of 1996 was passed, under the waiver rules available at the time to encourage research and evaluation of new approaches to welfare-to-work programs.)

The data used in this evaluation report came from twelve different sources:

- *Field research*, including interviews with program staff and observations of program activities throughout the study period;
- *Baseline data*, a one-page Background Information Form, completed when entering the study;
- *Unemployment insurance records*, to determine earnings from employment;
- *Public assistance records*, to determine cash assistance and food stamp amounts, and to track exemptions, sanctions, and other outcomes;
- *Three-year Client Survey*, which covered experiences of 2,424 clients approximately three years after their random assignment to the AFDC program or to the Jobs First program;
- *Teacher Survey*, of the teachers who taught children whose parents had filled out the Three-Year Client Survey;
- *Child care subsidy data*, to track amount of child care subsidy payments;
- *Safety Net program data*, to determine who was referred;
- *Fiscal records*, to determine overall program costs;
- *Interim client survey*, in 1998;
- *Staff surveys*; and
- *Post-time-limit surveys* of terminated clients three and six months after termination.

The client-level data came from cases in only two cities in Connecticut, New Haven and Manchester. They were chosen to represent two very different sets of circumstances.

New Haven, the third-largest city in the state, is one of the poorest cities in the United States: The median household income in 1990 was only about $26,000, and the poverty rate was about 21 percent. In contrast, Manchester covers a less populous, more suburban area near Hartford. In 1990, the median household income in Manchester was about $40,000, and the poverty rate was only 4 percent (Bloom et al., 2002, p. Sum-7).

Because this evaluation was intended to be comprehensive, the researchers wanted to ensure that they examined the implementation of the program, as well as the impacts. Data on implementation of program services and the institution of time limits came from some of the data sources noted earlier. Impacts were measured by comparing incomes, job characteristics, and other elements that were thought to be amenable to changes in welfare policy; and finally, the costs and benefits of the program were examined to determine if the benefits outweighed the costs.

Results and conclusions

This far-reaching evaluation had a host of results. This section will describe the findings in terms of implementation, outcome and efficiency.

Implementation

Clients in the Jobs First program were treated differently than those in the AFDC program. Jobs First clients heard a more employment-focused message than did the AFDC clients, and were also accurately informed about the program characteristics of Jobs First. Clients of the Jobs First program were more likely to participate in employment-related activities, particularly those leading to quick job placement. While this was in line with program expectations, because of implementation difficulties within the Jobs First program, the differences between the two programs in reality was not as great as it was expected to be.

Another aspect that was studied was the implementation of the time limits for welfare receipt, which, at 21 months, was one of the shortest in the nation. In practice, about two-thirds of clients who reached the time limit were given six-month extensions.

Outcomes

The evaluation report lists eleven separate findings under outcomes in the Summary Report (more findings exist in the full report). They are characterized here as positive (in keeping with program goals), negative (running counter to program goals), and mixed (with some positive and some negative aspects).

Positive Results. Compared to the AFDC group, Jobs First program participants were more likely to have a job and were less likely to be on welfare (Bloom et al., 2002, p. Sum-20). Contrary to fears of program critics, most of the work was full-time and stable in nature (p. Sum 22). Health care coverage increased significantly for adults (p. Sum-27). While there were not many effects on the variables of children's home environment, family functioning, and parenting practices, the significant effects were "generally positive" (p. Sum-29). Finally, child care was used more (p. Sum-27) and the increase in use was greatest among the lowest-income subgroup (p. Sum 31).

Negative Results. Compared to the AFDC group, the Jobs First program had no consistent effect on material well-being. The program did not significantly change levels of hardship felt by clients, which were high for both the AFDC and the Jobs First groups (p. Sum 25). Furthermore, Jobs First did not affect marital status or childbearing (p. Sum-27).

Mixed Results. The Jobs First program had no impact on school performance among elementary school children, but there was a small improvement on their behavior, particularly for the youngest students (p. Sum 29). For adolescents, the effects of being in the Jobs First program were negative for school performance (that is, they received lower grades) but family participation in Jobs First did lead to reductions in adolescents' involvement with police (p. Sum-29).

Efficiency. Only two results are mentioned in the area of the efficiency evaluation, and both are positive. First, although there was an additional cost to the Jobs First program compared to the AFDC program, it was only about $2,250 more per person over five years, or about $460 per person per year (p. Sum-31) which the authors say is lower than most other interventions with this population. Most important, the gains made by Job First clients were greater than program costs over five years (p. Sum-31).

Analyzing the Study. Given the length of the evaluation of Jobs First and the costs associated with the research, it is not surprising that the report is long and detailed. Still, long evaluations with many pages are not necessarily done well, so a systematic review of the project is still necessary to determine if the results merit being trusted. The analysis will look at sampling, measures, design, analysis, and interpretation, just as in the previous example.

Sampling

As the authors note in their summary, "almost all results in this report are drawn from the two research sites and thus may not represent the implementation or impacts of Jobs First in other offices in Connecticut" (Bloom et al., 2002, p. Sum-7). Given that the report gives the impression that the results are national in scope, because of the testing of many features of the welfare reform law (particularly the effects of time limits for welfare receipt) (Bloom et al., p. 3), it is very appropriate for the authors to point out this sampling problem.

The offices, one in New Haven and one in Manchester, are two out of the fifteen in the state. There were 3,513 clients from the New Haven office and 1,129 from the Manchester office who filled in the Background Information Form. The New Haven office, by itself, has nearly one-fourth of all the cases in the state. The office in Manchester serves about one-fourth as many cases as the New Haven office. In some ways, the populations served by the offices are similar: their age distribution and average age, the number of children per household, and the average age of the youngest child.

In most ways, however, the populations in the two cities are different. There are many more people of color in New Haven than Manchester (71% vs. 35%). About one-fifth (21%) of the New Haven caseload was employed at the time of their random assignment compared to 28% of the caseload in Manchester. In the New Haven office, 36% of the cases did not have a high school diploma or GED which was true of only 29% in the Manchester office. A greater percent of the caseload in New Haven was already receiving assistance when assigned compared to the Manchester office (65% to 52%). The list of differences between the two cities continues in the report (Bloom et al., 2002, pp. 18–19).

These differences are irrelevant, however, because the report does not compare these two cities to each other. It is important to note, however, that the clients in the study are only half of the clients who applied for welfare during the time of the study. This was done to "control the work-load for staff" (Bloom et al., 2002, p. 17). It is not entirely clear how the half to be in the study were chosen.

The report does not provide information showing that the cash-assistance population of these two offices was similar to that of the entire state. Given that two of the largest cities in the small state were selected, it is doubtful that the population is representative of other areas, which would be more rural and possibly have lower concentrations of people of color. Incomes, number of children, age of children, and so on, might be different in the 13 non-included offices than the two offices that were included. Because we do not know that the populations included in the two offices in the study are similar to the overall population of cash-assistance recipients in the state, it is better to assume that the results are not representative. Additionally, no comparisons to national statistics are provided, so the level of representativeness of that level is also unknown.

Measures

As noted above, the data for the evaluation came from twelve sources. The report provides considerable information regarding the details of each source (for example, see Box 6.2 in the report, which details the measures of "child care quality" and "stable child care"; p. 163). Some information was collected when clients were in the application process and some was collected later through interviews (in person or on the phone). Additional data were derived from administrative reports. The report indicates the strengths and weaknesses of administrative reports. Strengths include accuracy and availability on all clients. Weaknesses include being limited to activities in the state of Connecticut, and not including information on other members of the household (pp. 93–94).

In order to overcome these problems, another survey was conducted, which had its own set of problems. Three limitations are noted. First, because it happened nearly three years after the start of the experiment, people may have misremembered facts. Second, the survey response rate was only 80%. This is a good percentage in most surveys, yet the authors caution that there might be systematic differences between the respondents and non-respondents. Finally, the sample chosen for the survey was only half of the total study population (because of the cost of such surveys to administer), which leads to a decrease in confidence in its representativeness (Bloom et al., p. 94).

Due to the number of research questions, the sources of data needed to be many and varied. The evaluators recognized areas of strength in their measures but also areas of concern. To their credit, they took steps to fill in the holes of the data collection process and measures. This is an area of great strength for the evaluation.

Design

Earlier in this chapter, the comment was made that few true experiments occur in social policy evaluation. This example is an exception and automatically provides a considerable amount of trust in its quantitative findings, despite a full lack of generalizability caused by a lack of clear representativeness for the entire state from the people included in the data collection. The evaluation has random assignment to the new treatment condition (Jobs First program) and to the treatment-as-usual condition (AFDC program).

The authors were able to demonstrate that there were no systematic differences between the experimental treatment–receiving group and the treatment-as-usual group at the time of assignment. Both groups also experienced the same economic conditions, eliminating the threat of differential history. Other threats to internal validity were similarly taken care of by the experimental design.

One issue that was not controlled for, however, was the possible threat of contamination, meaning that some people in the control group received at least part of the experimental treatment. In Connecticut, before the start of the Jobs First program, the AFDC program was already moving to a greater emphasis on having clients work and to provide some services to enhance job-readiness. In addition, because the general tenor of the time was to encourage (if not mandate) work over welfare, the AFDC population most likely received a less intense version of the "work first" message that was more strongly promoted in the Jobs First program. The net effect of contamination is to weaken the observed differences in outcomes between the treatment and control groups, which would undercount the true impact of the Jobs First program.

Analysis

In some ways this study might be characterized as a mixed-methods evaluation rather than purely a quantitative study because of the care taken in researching the implementation of the program using interviews and other qualitative methods. It was chosen for this chapter because it exemplifies a true experimental design and great care was given to describing many of the aspects of the quantitative portions of the evaluation.

The interpretation of the implementation study (conducted primarily using interview techniques) suffers from the typical problems of qualitative analysis. Nonetheless, the descriptions of implementation problems experienced by staff seem well supported by comments and by quantitative data that provide triangulation of information.

Unfortunately, the quantitative data analysis presented in the report is not sufficiently sophisticated. The most commonly shown statistics were percentages and means. Statistical tests to determine differences between the treatment and the control groups were limited to two-tailed t-tests. In a somewhat unconventional move, precise significance levels were not provided. Asterisks were used instead, with *** indicating significant at the .01 level, ** at the .05 level, and * at the .10 level (this information is buried in the small print at the bottom of tables; see, for example, p. 145, the bottom of Table 5.7, although it holds true for every table using statistical tests). Including the .10 level as a significant result without emphasizing that doing so is unusual within the context of most social sciences seems an underhanded way of inflating the number of significant results in the study. No corrections were employed to take into account the large numbers of t-tests made. In addition, bivariate analysis does not examine the interactions between more than two variables at a time. While a t-test is an appropriate statistical measure to compare two means, more advanced techniques should have been used to model the data in multivariate ways. Another way to improve the data analysis would be to have calculated effect sizes rather than relying on repeated use of the t-test (Mindel and Hoefer, 2006).

The benefit-cost analysis is well described and its limitations are noted (pp. 215–216). In most regards, this aspect of the results seems quite credible. Still, it is disappointing that tests of significance were not performed to determine if differences existed between the Jobs First and the AFDC populations in the areas of earnings, fringe benefits, and personal taxes (Bloom et al., 2002, p. 217).

To summarize this section, the analysis is mediocre. Given the positive comments relating to the measures and design, it was anticipated that more would be done with the vast amounts of data gathered. One might be able to forgive the non-representativeness of the sampling if there had been some exceptional analysis for the population in the study. This, however, did not occur.

Interpretation

Because it has taken several pages to go through the analysis of sampling, measures, design, and analysis, a summary may be helpful. In short, the sampling seemed unrepresentative of the state, the measures were appropriate and well-described; the design was excellent; and the analysis was rather lackluster, at best.

The problems, then, with the sampling and the analysis cause the interpretation of the results to be unreliable. Using an alpha of .10 rather than .05 to determine significance undercuts the analytical section, particularly as this decision is neither mentioned in the body of the report nor justified. Of special note is the use of only bivariate analysis of impact. By not holding a large number of variables constant simultaneously through multivariate analysis (a common enough procedure in 2002, widely taught and practiced in policy analysis and evaluation circles), all of the interpretation is suspect.

CONCLUSION

This chapter has covered the basics of quantitative policy analysis and program evaluation. Information relating to design and data collection and analysis has been presented, and two examples of welfare reform research have been analyzed using the concepts presented in the chapter. It has been emphasized that the evaluation process should be systematic and rigorous. In this way, we have noted that even expensive and extensive evaluations may have flaws that are easy to gloss over if one is not paying attention to the details.

The next chapter takes looks at mixed-methods evaluations, those that combine qualitative and quantitative methods to overcome the potential limitations of each. The pairing of the methods also underscores the importance of having familiarity with a broad range of research methodologies to be able to conduct strong policy analyses and program evaluations.

7

Using Mixed Methods to Understand What the Policy Did

The previous two chapters have covered the two families of data-gathering techniques in policy analysis: qualitative methods and quantitative methods. The advantages and disadvantages of both have been discussed, as have specific techniques associated with these broad categories of methods. After that, examples of studies using the measurement approach were presented, in some detail, to point out the range of strengths and weaknesses that may be encountered in the process of using them in the real world. This chapter combines qualitative and quantitative methods into what is called *mixed-methods research* and presents information on this approach to policy research and program evaluation.

DESCRIPTION OF THE MIXED-METHODS APPROACH TO SOCIAL POLICY EVALUATION

It is helpful to begin the discussion of mixed methods by stipulating that both qualitative and quantitative research methods are useful and that the differences between them are often overstated in a bid to "one-up" adherents of the other style. No matter the case many years ago, it seems apparent that currently, Read and Marsh (2002) are correct in stating that "evidence from research practice suggests that the traditional philosophical division between quantitative and qualitative methods is increasingly being viewed as a false dichotomy" (p. 235). London, Schwartz, and Scott (2006) echo this sentiment from their own experience, arguing that "the integration of quantitative and qualitative research methodologies and data holds great promise for enhancing the evaluation of policies and programs" (p. 352).

One of the keys to understanding the emerging potential of mixed-methods research is to remember that, to be effective, the research or evaluation effort must always be approached systematically and with attention to the details that make the difference between achieving something worthwhile and something that emerges as a waste of time and resources. It is not the case that one can create a competent mixed-methods study by inappropriately combining poorly understood techniques and under-trained staff. Both qualitative and quantitative research have guidelines for doing research "correctly" that should be followed, even when combining the methods to answer a single set of research questions in one study.

Read and Marsh (2002) note that there are two main reasons for using a mixed-methods design. The first reason is that sometimes the research topic cannot be fully explored using only one type of method. The second reason is that the two types of methods used together increase validity and trustworthiness by serving as checks on each other (p. 237). This can be conceptualized as methodological "triangulation," using more than one way to measure a concept. In mixed-methods research, this is particularly effective if one uses qualitative and quantitative measures together to measure the same phenomenon (Read and Marsh, pp. 237–238).

The combination of the two approaches to measurement can occur in at least three different ways (Creswell, 1994, cited in Read and Marsh, 2002, p. 239). The first is to implement a two-phase process. Each stage is "true to its school" of thought regarding the data collection and write-up and informs the other style of research without being particularly connected. In the end, the results are more or less appended to each other without much integration. Padgett (2008) pays close attention to the ordering of the two stages. If the qualitative methods component comes first, then it is usually considered "exploratory," and the results are used to improve the subsequent quantitative methods, usually by deepening the understanding of options for the quantitative study component. This is common in terms of designing survey questions or other measures during a pre-testing phase. For example, in developing a question related to how low-income people make it from month to month, the researcher can ask this in an open-ended way in order to develop a listing that captures all of the options ever mentioned, which might include some items that never would have emerged otherwise. The researcher thus gains the advantage of greater validity and trustworthiness because the questions asked are more in line with the respondents' reality.

When the stages are reversed, and the quantitative results are gathered first, they often become the basis of the qualitative study, providing the starting point of an important conversation. The evaluators can perform quantitative analysis, but, recognizing that averages, standard deviations, and t-tests do not tell the entire story, they may then talk with the respondents, asking them questions along the lines of, "We see this pattern emerging in the data. What do you think of it? How does that interpretation fit with *your* life?"

Creswell (1994) argues that the mixing of qualitative and quantitative methods might be more or less complete. Sometimes one method dominates the other, with the subordinate method being used to partially cover the weaknesses of the dominant approach. The other situation Creswell describes is when both methods are used in a complementary and equal way, actively involved in the same process. This approach can be used at any time in the research process, although the sooner the approach is planned for, the better the outcome. It takes considerable effort to integrate the two approaches so that the most is made of their combined use.

PLANNING FOR USING MIXED-METHODS RESEARCH METHODS IN SOCIAL POLICY EVALUATION

There are not any specific research methods found in the mixed-methods category that are not in either the qualitative or quantitative schools of thought. However, London et al. (2006) describe the importance of planning for the mixed-methods approach. They specify that greater emphasis should be put on the planning aspects of mixed-methods research "so that research questions and instruments can be coordinated from the outset and fielded in tandem" (p. 351). Part of the planning is to ensure that the sample of respondents used for the qualitative efforts is embedded and linked with the quantitative sample. Thus, if a broad quantitative survey were to be fielded in a community, a portion of that sample could also be chosen for the more in-depth qualitative aspects as well. Their comments and insights would then be directly relevant to the larger survey results as they would be a part of the larger survey (London et al., 2006). Another unique aspect of the planning process for mixed-methods research is that the same evaluators should work on both the quantitative and the qualitative data analysis (London et al., p. 351). This is the best way to increase the chances of cross-fertilization of information across the qualitative/quantitative divide.

ADVANTAGES OF THE MIXED-METHODS APPROACH TO SOCIAL POLICY EVALUATION

The main advantage of using mixed methods, as has been alluded to previously, is that the evaluation is better with the use of both types of methodologies than either is by itself. As noted, which component comes first, second, or whether these come at the same time, depends on the research questions to be answered. In general, if done well, the choice to combine the two approaches will help evaluators develop more complete knowledge of the intervention and its effects.

Additionally, the inclusion of both quantitative and qualitative information can make the results of the evaluation more convincing to different types of readers. Some decision-makers and stakeholders are more persuaded by the "hard facts" that emerge from quantitative methods. Others find that client or staff narratives are more powerful for shaping their views of the program's worth. As a researcher or evaluator, it is impossible to know in advance which type of information will be more valuable to the varied readers who will encounter the final report. It may thus be a good strategy to build in "something for everyone" if part of the aim of the research is to make convincing recommendations for program continuation, demolition, or growth.

CRITIQUES OF THE MIXED-METHODS APPROACH TO SOCIAL POLICY EVALUATION

Despite the advantages of the mixed-methods approach, there are some problematic areas. First, if the quantitative and qualitative research method paradigms are truly as important as some believe, then it may be difficult to have one person do both the qualitative and the quantitative research efforts. Most researchers have a clear bias in their training and preferences regardless of their philosophical positions, and it may be difficult to overcome one's training as a quantitative or qualitative researcher in order to become competent in using the methods of "the other." One way around this problem is to use a research team approach, combining the efforts of open-minded specialists in the different methodological approaches. In the best cases, a true synergy will be attained. In the worst cases, there will be lively discussions. Another solution on the horizon is that more doctoral programs are focusing on a balanced training in both qualitative and quantitative methods to prepare researchers for conducting mixed-methods research.

The use of triangulation in measurement is almost always considered good practice, and so it is with mixed-methods research, where the two different approaches usually provide valuable and interesting reinforcement to the main findings of the other approach. At times, however, it may be that the findings contradict each other. In this case, the discussions may get extremely lively, as the evaluators try to understand the disagreement in results and discuss whether the disparities are related to the actual situation or whether they are caused by the methodologies themselves.

One final barrier to mixed-methods research is the comparative cost disadvantage. Both types of research and evaluation can be expensive to do well. To include the further dimension of a qualitative component to a quantitative study, or vice versa, adds significantly to the cost of the project.

None of these points should be sufficient to stop the movement towards awareness of the increased value of using a mixed-methods data collection strategy compared to a single approach. Still, these potential problems must be acknowledged, and plans should be laid out to overcome them before the project begins.

USING MIXED METHODS IN RESEARCHING TANF OUTCOMES

As we have done in the previous two chapters, this section lays out an analysis of two mixed-methods evaluations of specific aspects of welfare reform. The analytical criteria we use are a combination of the criteria used in the chapter regarding qualitative methods and also those used in the chapter on quantitative methods, in addition to those mentioned in this chapter. Because mixed methods is a relatively new approach to research, and there are no specific methods for policy analysis using mixed methods, locating a study on welfare reform that balanced the focus on qualitative and quantitative data was not possible. In lieu of this, two studies are presented: the first in Indiana, which looks at the full result of the welfare reform efforts there; and the second from a study of a program in Wisconsin designed to provide additional supports to families transitioning from welfare to work.

Example 1:

E. Beecroft, W. Lee, and D. Long (2003): *The Indiana Welfare Reform Evaluation: Five Year Impacts, Implementation, Costs and Benefits.* Cambridge, Mass.: Abt Associates. Retrieved from http://www.abtassociates.com/reports/indiana_final_report.pdf.

Background and Research Objectives

Indiana began its welfare reform efforts under a waiver granted by the federal government in 1995, before the passage of the Personal Responsibility and Work Opportunity Reconciliation Act of 1996. The Indiana plan, called "Partnership for Personal Responsibility" (Partnership), was implemented with evaluation in mind. In 1995, approximately 95% of the AFDC caseload of over 66,000 families in all of the state's 92 counties was randomly assigned to be subject to the new rules, and the other 5% remained on the then-current AFDC program. (This was changed later on so that random assignment was used in only 12 counties, and 20% of those applying were selected for the AFDC rules.) The program goals were "to increase clients' employment and decrease their reliance on welfare, to make work more financially rewarding than public assistance, and to encourage responsible parenting" (Beecroft et al., 2003, p. vi). Of considerable interest in terms of the program's design is that adult recipients received an eligibility time limit of only 24 months.

Between the start of the program in 1995 and the 2003 report, the program remained substantially the same, with the same goals, although the economic conditions that low-income people had to cope with changed a great deal in Indiana as in the rest of the country. Indiana state government also experienced considerable fluctuation in its economic fortunes, including lower tax revenue with which to fund the state share of TANF program costs. The evaluation report addressed two primary questions:

- How has Indiana's welfare reform program affected participating families, and have those effects changed over time?
- Has the program been cost-effective? (Beecroft et al., 2003, p. vi).

The program report characterizes the entire evaluation as having a process component as well as client outcome and cost-benefit aspects. The particular evaluation questions for the process evaluation (that is, the examination of "the program's planning, design and operation with an eye towards identifying places where intended and actual operations may differ") (Beecroft et al., 2003, p. 10) were:

- What are the major components of the demonstration design, and what were they intended to accomplish?
- How were the major components of the welfare reform plan implemented at the local level? How different are the experiences of the Welfare Reform and Traditional Welfare groups in terms of services and program requirements?
- How did the welfare reform demonstration evolve over time? What implementation problems arose, and how were these problems addressed? How fully were the major components implemented? What are the implications for program impacts? (Beecroft et al., 2003, p. 10).

The authors list four particular questions for the adult outcomes (outcomes for children are described in a separate report):

- Did welfare reform affect welfare and food stamp receipt?
- Did welfare reform affect employment and earnings?
- What impact did the program have on household income?

- Did impacts differ for particular subgroups of clients? (Beecroft et al., 2003, p. 10)

The benefit-cost analysis in the study answered the question of whether the benefits of the programmatic change were greater than the costs of the program. Because the answer to this question often depends on the viewpoint of different actors, the report addresses the question from three different perspectives: that of the families on welfare, of government at the state and national level, and of society as a whole.

Methods used

The evaluation of Indiana's welfare reform efforts used a classic experimental design, employing random assignment into a control (AFDC) group and a treatment (Partnership) group. All 66,440 families who were either currently in the program or who applied during welfare reform's first year were used in the initial evaluation plan. Thus, any potential problem concerning external generalizability to other families on welfare in Indiana was eliminated. The initial treatment group included 63,223 families, while the control group had 3,217 families. Regression analysis indicated that there were only slight, insignificant differences on key variables between the randomly assigned groups at baseline.

The evaluation had several components. The evaluation examined implementation efforts in several ways: by observation at local offices and the central office (in 1996, 1998, and 2001); through telephone interviews and mail surveys of program staff (administrators and case workers); and with client focus groups. The cost-benefit portion of the evaluation used administrative record data from the program, state unemployment insurance system records, and a follow-up survey of clients after five years to determine benefits. The evaluation examined expenditure records from the program's financial management office to calculate costs.

Over the course of the evaluation, some policy changes were made to make the transition from welfare to work somewhat easier. Thus, the later entrants into the welfare system faced a somewhat more beneficent environment than did the initial program participants. The report describes a smaller, special follow-up research effort at the end of the evaluation to capture possible differences among clients by looking at a subset of participants who entered the program during the last two years. This study included 4,954 families from 12 counties, with 3,863 families assigned to the Partnership program group and 1,091 families assigned to the AFDC group.

The authors chose to include as significant results any findings that were less than .10, and all tests of differences between averages were based on two-tailed tests, since the results could be either positive or negative.

Results and Conclusions

The report had a considerable number of results. They will be presented only briefly, broken into implementation and process results, outcome results, and cost-benefit results.

Implementation and process results

The evaluation of the implementation of the program makes good use of both quantitative and qualitative results to determine how well the program was implemented, where things went well, and where problems existed. The underlying basis of the report is quantitative, but these results are illuminated with information from surveys and in-person interviews of staff.

The first few findings indicate that the program was implemented as intended (Beecroft et al., 2003, p. 19), which included a strong work-first model (p. 20). Over time, difficulties were encountered in staff division of responsibilities, primarily in that the eligibility and case-management functions were separated, causing client and staff difficulties. As a result, these two functions were combined (p. 20). This switch caused problems as well, however, as the "integrated" workers continued to spend most of their time on determining eligibility and little on the "case coordination" aspects of their clients' cases. This caused the case workers a great deal of frustration. This finding was first noticed using quantitative measures of worker job satisfaction and later was asked about using open-ended survey questions. Interestingly, the case workers vividly described the problem of work overload, while "central office staff and some local-level management staff" were much more likely to believe that the case coordinators could have done a better job of balancing the two duties they were tasked with (Beecroft et al., 2003, p. 27).

The large changes to the welfare program in Indiana led to changes in program structure and implementation patterns. Two aspects of this were noted by Beecroft et al. (2003). First, the new program caused devolution from the state level to localities, and then to contracting out of program responsibilities (p. 21); and the contracting-out process was adapted over time to be more effective (p. 21). The use of performance-based contracting (rather than fee-for-service payments) was an important element of the change, causing rippling effects through the system of state government, local government, and contracting organizations. Too much emphasis on performance indicators that were far in the future (such as job retention) created financial burdens on the contractors, so changes were made in order for the organizations to be paid for up-front tasks, such as assessments and ongoing mentoring.

Implementation analysis looked at the use of support services such as transportation and child care programs, as well as Medicaid. A considerable number of clients used all of the programs, and client interviews elicited their opinion of the necessity for these supports. One client is quoted as saying: "Child care and transportation—that's the most important [work-related service] because without transportation you can't get to your job and without child care you can't go to your job" (Beecroft et al., 2003, p. 45). While policy-makers, staff, and clients expressed their belief in the value of these services, fiscal problems at the state level imperiled their continuation at the end of the evaluation time frame.

Outcome Results

The quantitative elements of the research are strongest in this section and the next, the cost-benefit analysis. The results provided by the larger study of all families are examined first. Three of the key results of welfare reform in Indiana are that a smaller number of people received both welfare checks (TANF) and food stamps after five years; government spent less on TANF and food stamps after five years; and TANF program recipients, on average, increased their earnings and employment rates in each of the follow-up years compared to AFDC families (Beecroft et al., 2003, p. 68). For people working, their jobs tended to be full time and at wages above minimum wage. In addition, income for two-adult households increased (Beecroft et al., p. 69). Welfare reform in Indiana, however, did not affect total income for single-adult families (Beecroft et al., p. 69). Although some critics believed that health insurance coverage rates would drop once families were no longer eligible for TANF, policies put into place meant that there was no significant effect in either direction (Beecroft et al., p. 69).

Turning to the results of the smaller study that was completed using families in only 12 counties who enrolled in TANF after several more lenient policies were begun, we find that TANF payment impacts were larger than for the earlier group after the second year, but this impact faded in later years, probably because AFDC recipients were able to retain more of their work income due to a policy change. This made it more "profitable" for AFDC program clients to work than before, thus reducing the difference between them and the TANF recipients who were put into a work-first environment once they became a client (Beecroft et al., 2003, p. 93). The experimental program also increased the rate of employment among recipients but did not increase earnings to a significant extent in the two years studied (p. 93). Finally, just as with the full-scale study, there were no impacts on total income (earnings, welfare payments, and food stamp benefits) (p. 93).

Cost-benefit analysis

Beecroft et al. (2003) make three empirically based statements in this section of the report regarding the effectiveness of welfare reform in Indiana from the perspective of the families, government, and society. First, the average single-adult family was in a slightly better financial position after welfare reform. The economic benefit to this average family resulted primarily from working more hours for more pay (p. 104). While the average family was better off, some families were worse off. Second, savings to government (state and national) from lower TANF, food stamps, and Medicaid costs were greater than the increased costs of the welfare reform components, such as training and employment services, child care, transportation, and so on. Third, as a consequence of these two cost-benefit elements, "the estimated benefits to society of Indiana's welfare reform program exceed its costs by several thousand dollars per welfare family" (Beecroft et al., 2003, p. 104).

Summary of results

The overall picture painted by these results is, at worst, modestly positive for the average family on TANF, in general, and compared to the AFDC recipient families in particular. Welfare reform appears to be better than having retained the older system.

Yet the authors also acknowledge that the program in Indiana has not solved the problems of low-income families. Many families are not better off, even if they are not worse off. After five years of welfare reform, "most families were still struggling" (p. xii). These families possibly still had incomes below the poverty line (60%), were food "insecure" (40%), and had used food banks at least once in the previous 12 months (20%). Other indicators of struggle were mothers being at heightened risk of clinical depression (40%) and domestic violence (25%). Being poor in Indiana, as is true all over America, means being insecure and at risk. The authors poignantly state, "Evidence from other states suggests similar levels of disadvantage among single-parent families on welfare. Welfare reform alone is not a cure-all for families receiving welfare" (p. xii).

Analyzing the Study

While the summary of the evaluation presented here does not do it full justice, two items quickly emerge while reading the report. First, the authors do a very nice job of interweaving the qualitative aspects of the evaluation with the quantitative. Certainly, the focus is on the quantitative data and their analysis, yet the research report finds ways to add the voices of staff members and clients to the mix, allowing us to understand better what the numbers mean. While this could have been done to an even greater extent, the authors of this report have produced other manuscripts that can be turned to for additional detail and insights (see, for example, Beecroft, Cahill, and Goodson, 2002; and Lee et al., 2003).

Sampling, Representativeness, Generalizability, and Extrapolation

In this case, when, for one of the surveys, every family in the welfare system is included, the ideas of sampling and representativeness are irrelevant. The main evaluation information, then, of the first-year cohort need not worry about being representative—it just is what it is, because it is the population being studied. One might also quibble about the size of the two groups—control and treatment—being so unequal, but the random assignment and equal averages across the two groups make this a very small concern. The concept of representativeness is more relevant in discussing the implementation and process evaluation components. On the positive side, all counties in the state were included in the field visits. There is less information about how the offices were selected, how staff members in each office were chosen to be surveyed or interviewed, and the process of choosing which clients to have in focus groups.

For the second major data-collection effort, of families who came into the welfare system after it had been implemented for three years, there is more to question in terms of representativeness. Recall that only 12 counties were used. Information on how these dozen counties were chosen is not provided, although it is intimated that they may have been selected because they were the largest counties. If so, then smaller and more rural counties were definitely not well represented. For the qualitative aspects of the study, there is no indication that focus groups were conducted until saturation and redundancy were achieved, leading to questions regarding the representativeness of the varied realities of those studied.

Measures/Reliability, Trustworthiness through Triangulation, and Transparency

The authors go to considerable length to describe the measures employed in this evaluation. The many research questions asked over a five-year period mean that there were a large number of concepts measured. Some of the things measured for the implementation and process evaluation included the number of clients who participated in employment and training activities, what types of employment and training activities clients participated in, the use of sanctions of various types, and so on. Personnel issues such as job tenure and job satisfaction were also measured. Measures relating to the outcome component of the evaluation were even more numerous. A few that were highly important included hours of work, length of job tenure, rate of pay, type of job obtained, health insurance coverage, food stamp use, et cetera.

Quantitative measures were provided at the descriptive level. While there was some use of t-tests to compare averages, these merely described the data. Inferential statistics and modeling were not employed (see the section on analysis, below). Qualitative data providing method triangulation and source triangulation were also present. However, little was noted regarding triangulation of analysts related to the five-year-impacts portion of the evaluation and their possible biases in the analysis process.

Design

The experimental evaluation design for both the main five-year data collection effort and the second survey, covering only two years, is extremely impressive, and eliminates almost all threats to internal validity.

The authors noted that there was probably some transfer of program effort to the AFDC clients simply because the clients were in the same offices as the Partnership program participants and had the same staff members. Also, at least some of the clients on AFDC rules believed that they were supposed to operate under the rules of the welfare reform program.

Validity/Confirmability/Objectivity

The authors provided a fair description of their evaluation plans and compared the results, at times, to other research about welfare reform efforts in other states. The data seem to have been collected using appropriate instruments, particularly administrative data. While it is true that administrative record data can be inappropriately selected and used simply because they are convenient, in this case it appears that the measures were closely related to the concepts to be evaluated. Because not very much information is known regarding the questions and procedures used in the process evaluation and client focus groups, it is not as easy to ascertain the amount of credibility to give to them, other than face validity.

Data analysis

The quantitative analysis seems to have been done properly, although the selection of an alpha level of .10 for statistical significance seems unnecessarily lenient, given the large number of cases involved and the relative ease of achieving statistical significance in such circumstances. The use of effect size would be more helpful, as it would show the level of impact rather than the odds that the results were due to chance (Mindel and Hoefer, 2006). Additional analysis using multivariate analysis would have improved understanding of the data as well. Bivariate tests cannot hold other variables constant and can lead to believing that results are important, even though they are really due to spurious relationships. There is no description of how qualitative data were analyzed.

Interpretation

The quantitative data analysis is very straightforward, given that the numbers are descriptive, not inferential. It is not difficult to interpret means and frequency counts. The use of comparison results from other states also provides an air of correctness in understanding the results. Yet, this evaluation falls prey to the same problems noted in the previous chapter's analysis of the welfare reform efforts in Connecticut: the repeated bivariate analysis efforts are simply a poor substitute for a single regression or Structural Equation Modeling (SEM) procedure.

The use of quotes from focus group participants and interviews with staff to underscore the quantitative results adds to the feeling that the authors were validly interpreting the quantitative data, at least as far as they took it. There is no separate and systematic analysis of the qualitative data, and there is not much interpretation presented. Because of this, it is hard to argue that the interpretation is correct or incorrect. It seems a waste of the material gathered to not place more emphasis on it.

Example 2:

L. Bernheimer, T. Weisner, and E. Lowe (2003): Impacts of children with troubles on working poor families: Mixed-method and experimental evidence. *Mental Retardation, 11*(6): 403–419.

Background and Research Objectives

New Hope was a welfare-to-work program in Milwaukee, Wisconsin, that included the first three years of implementation of the PRWORA. New Hope benefits included "(a) a wage supplement (to ensure that income remained above the poverty threshold for their family), (b) subsidies for affordable health insurance, (c) child care vouchers, and (d) a full-time community service job opportunity for those unable to find work on their own" (Bernheimer et al., 2003, p. 404). As part of the evaluation of New Hope, Bernheimer et al. conducted a mixed-methods study "to understand the effects of a child with troubles on the family" (p. 404), focusing on the impact of PRWORA work requirements on the family's routine with and without New Hope benefits.

Of specific focus was whether the New Hope program assisted the family in developing sustainable routines; i.e., routines that "(a) fit current resources, (b) reflect balance among competing and often conflicting family interests, (c) are stable over time, and (d) reflect the pursuit and achievement of meaningful family goals and values" given

PRWORA work requirements (p. 404). The guiding questions were: "(a) What is the type and prevalence of child troubles in the Ethnographic Study? (b) What was the experimental impact of New Hope on families with and without troubled children? (c) What is the relationship between child troubles and sustainability of the daily routine?" (Bernheimer et al., 2003, p. 408).

Methods used

This was a mixed-methods study that employed an experimental design. Families had to meet four criteria to participate: "(a) have lived in one of the two targeted neighborhoods in Milwaukee, (b) been older than 18, (c) had an income at or below 150% of the poverty line, and (d) been willing to work 30 or more hours a week" (Bernheimer et al., 2003, 404). A total of 745 families were randomly assigned to New Hope ($n = 366$) or a control group ($n = 371$); these families each had at least one child who was between the age of one and 10 at the beginning of the study. Both groups were allowed to utilize federal and state public assistance; those in the experimental group had the additional New Hope benefits.

The qualitative portion of the study utilized ethnography to gain an understanding of New Hope's impact. The ethnography used a stratified random sample of 42 families (21 experimental and 21 control). The focus was on participants' "lives, their concerns and hopes, and their everyday routines," especially as they related to "work experiences, child care and child monitoring, take up and use of the New Hope offer, roles of fathers and partners in mothers' lives, family finances, and beliefs about the welfare system" (Bernheimer et al., p. 406). Each family had multiple contacts (interviews and observations) with fieldworkers, with the first contact encouraging families to "tell their story" (Bernheimer et al., p. 406). Remaining contacts were designed to draw out more information about those stories as they related to the project.

Surveys and administrative records for the 745 families focused on non–New Hope services used, economic outcomes (hours of work, hourly wages, the type of jobs held; welfare payments, food stamps, Medicaid benefits, and receipt of earned income tax credits), and non-economic outcomes related to family well-being (Bernheimer et al., 2003, p. 405) providing the quantitative data for the study. Additional quantitative data were extracted from field notes taken during the ethnographic portion of the study, including a "child troubles" score assessment of family sustainability, and a "family-level troubles" score.

Results and Conclusions

The authors of this report provide a large number of results, in some detail, so this overview is necessarily incomplete. Still, it will provide the gist of the needed information. Data in the study support previous research that low-income families have a higher rate of children with disabilities than other families. Additionally, the data imply that the rate may be higher (about 33%) than documented, as ethnographic data identified children with issues (e.g., health, behavior, academic performance) that were not identified by some formal organization (e.g., schools). However, the data do not support the assumption that having children with troubles alone is a barrier to employment, with only 16% of the families in the study with child troubles having this as the sole barrier to employment. Rather, the data indicate that it is the burden of many strains that creates a cumulative effect hindering parents' abilities to acquire and maintain employment. The authors note: "In conclusion, low-income families with children who have significant disabilities and other learning and behavior troubles comprise a population that deserves special consideration from a policy perspective" (p. 415). Furthermore, "children with serious mental, emotional, and behavioral disorders as well as respiratory problems have been disproportionately represented among those losing benefits (Luprest, 1996; Ohlson, 1998; Rosman and Knitzer, 2001)" (p. 415), further challenging low-income families with regard to developing sustainable family routines necessary for stable employment. In terms of policy-oriented solutions, Bernheimer et al. (2003) conclude that New Hope is one example of operationalizing this special consideration.

> Additional benefits would assist this population, including waivers from work where indicated, along with improved home care options for parents. These parents would benefit from more flexible work, including time to take telephone calls and attend school conferences. They need health care, school services, and family services. In many cases, the 'problem' is as much a service problem (lack of available services) and job site problem (absence of work flexibility, no child care, and/or no health benefits), as it is a child, parent, or family adaptive problem (Bernheimer et al., 2003, pp. 415–416).

Analyzing the Study

Again, the summary of this evaluation presented here is brief, but one will quickly note that the authors are very aware of the ways the qualitative and quantitative data work together to inform policy. The authors emphasize the qualitative data and their analysis, yet they find ways to extract, quantitatively, the nuances of the plethora of data produced from the 402 ethnographic contacts with families, painting a rich and detailed picture of these families' experiences without losing the rich essences captured by the qualitative. There is more information from this study that is described elsewhere due to the sheer amount of data collected (see, for example, Bos et al., 1999).

Sampling, Representativeness, Generalizability, and Extrapolation

The concept of representativeness is important when sampling from a population in order to obtain results that are similar to the entire population's. In this case, for the quantitative surveys conducted with the 745 families and the ethnographic portion with the 42 families, random sampling was used, ensuring representativeness within the limits of random error and the possibility of excess attrition. While this assuages the quantitative concern of generalizability, it leaves unanswered questions regarding qualitative extrapolation. In terms of representativeness and extrapolation, the qualitative researcher aims to ensure "representativeness" of participants' realities through theoretical sampling until saturation and redundancy are achieved. Because the researchers used an unusually large sample size for the ethnographic portion of this study (Sandelowski, 1995), it is highly plausible that, had they theoretically sampled beyond the 42 families, they would have realized they had achieved saturation and redundancy. However, because this step was not taken, we cannot be sure.

Measures/Reliability, Trustworthiness through Triangulation, and Transparency

The report provides comprehensive descriptions of the measures used, especially the quantitative ones derived from qualitative data. Unfortunately, the full possibilities of these quantitative data are not fully explored, as the analysis of this information is only descriptive.

Although some correlations are noted, the analysis does not include any inferential statistics or modeling of outcomes of interest.

The use of mixed methods and large samples for the qualitative and quantitative portions provides triangulation of sources and methods, providing opportunities for qualitative and quantitative data to be used for comparative confirmation of results. Additionally, the study employs multiple levels of analyst triangulation, with the authors triangulating with each other and with the fieldworkers who gathered the ethnographic data. However, the authors do not address issues of transparency, omitting information about their own possible biases and those of their field workers in terms of how that might affect their analysis.

Design

Having a random sample for both the larger sample used for the survey and for the smaller sample for the ethnographic portion is a strong point of this evaluation, with random sampling being extremely rare in qualitative research. It is rare for a few reasons, but pragmatically because it is often difficult to identify a sampling frame from which to draw a sample. Having a random sample eliminates many of the internal threats to validity. However, aside from attrition, the authors do not address other issues of internal validity such as instrumentation, experimenter bias, and compensatory rivalry or resentful demoralization between the experimental and control groups.

Validity/Confirmability/Objectivity

Bernheimer et al. (2003) describe their evaluation activities well. They provide results of a few other studies of the working poor for comparison purposes. Their data collection methods are appropriate. The authors also go into great detail regarding how they derived quantitative measures from qualitative data; however, little detail is provided about the quantitative survey. It is more difficult to assess the quality of the survey because so little information is given about it. The readers do not know what the specific questions in the survey were, nor what procedures were used to gather the information. Levels of validity, confirmability, and objectivity are thus difficult to determine. Perhaps the two key strengths of this study related to these concepts are the use of mixed methods and of multiple analysts, providing a multitude of data sources and analysis perspectives.

Data Analysis

The analysis seems to have been done properly. It could be argued that the selection of an alpha level of .05 for statistical significance is unnecessarily stringent, given the exploratory nature of the study and the relatively small sample size ($n = 42$) utilized for the correlations. Still, this alpha level is often considered the default level for social science research, so the authors are following convention. The reader is left with questions as to why the survey data gathered from the 745 families in the experimental and control groups were not also analyzed. Though mentioned in the "Method" section of the article, results were not reported, with quantitative data being solely those derived from the qualitative ethnographic interactions. Additional analysis of the survey data using multivariate analysis would have improved our understanding of the data.

Interpretation

The authors give themselves an easy job in interpreting the quantitative results, which are descriptive in nature. Frequency counts, averages, and correlations are understood by readers without much difficulty. It is helpful to have the results that are included in the report from other studies to provide information on how this state's experiences compare to what occurred in other places. The authors do interject quotes from ethnographic interactions with participants into their narrative, and this adds credence to the interpretation of the quantitative data. Still, the report does not go beyond the simplest of quantitative analysis techniques and thus cannot provide the level of understanding that even slightly more advanced multivariate techniques could provide. The interpretation presented thus seems much shallower than it could be. A great deal of meaning in the data is left unexplored and so there is definitely an underutilization of the possibilities in this type of mixed-methods study.

CONCLUSION

The use of mixed methods and the rationale for doing so is described in this chapter. The potential for improving both qualitative and quantitative evaluations is considerable when both are done correctly. In the case of the first example, while the use of open-ended questions in surveys, interviews, and focus groups with stakeholders adds a richer voice to the bare averages and frequencies, the qualitative aspects of the evaluation cannot fully save the evaluation from the problems of limited and low-level data analysis. Likewise, the limited attention to the nuances of qualitative research leaves questions regarding trustworthiness, objectivity, and confirmability. The second example has similar difficulties. Though the authors pay sufficient attention to trustworthiness, their treatment of the quantitative data is less than adequate. In short, there is much promise in mixed-methods research for policy evaluation that has not yet been realized.

8

Conclusion: Using Social Policy Creation and Evaluation

This book's stated purpose is to provide an understanding of how to use decision-making models to understand the policy that is enacted and how to evaluate the effects of those policies. In effect, the book has examined the alpha and the omega of policy-making, leaving aside the many other aspects of the policy process. We have now come to the end, so let us review what has been covered and try to tie up any loose ends that might remain.

DECISION-MAKING MODELS OF POLICY CREATION

Three different models were presented discussing the decisions made in passing the Personal Responsibility and Work Opportunities Reconciliation Act of 1996. The first, dubbed the "historical approach," examined the passage as a culmination of historical events and trends, focusing on how the 1996 law was a continuation of the debates on welfare policy throughout history. If we listen, we hear echoes of the controversy over who should receive public support and who should not, what level of support should be provided, and what the best level of government is to provide that support. These topics can be traced back to at least the Elizabethan Poor Law of 1601. Terms such as *deserving poor* (vs. *undeserving poor*), the principle of less eligibility, and federalism encapsulate the meanings of these debates that have extended over considerable time periods.

The deserving poor are those who are poor through no fault of their own, such as widows and children. But the definition of "deserving" changes with time and circumstance. At times, the elderly are placed in this category as well, although in recent years there is a tendency to say that retired persons should have saved more during their working years so that they would not be poor now. Usually, people with disabilities also are considered deserving of support; yet, with the advent of the Americans with Disabilities Act (ADA), people with disabilities are not only being allowed to compete for jobs on a more equal basis, but are increasingly being required to work if possible. On the other side of the coin, it is almost always true that healthy males of working age are considered the *undeserving poor*, that is, undeserving of public support. These people should be working to earn their own wages and to take care of any family members they may have.

The idea of *less eligibility* is simply that the level of benefits provided to the poor should be less than the least amount of wages that can be earned through working. It should always be more lucrative to work than to receive welfare. If not, then a moral hazard exists in that people may willingly become dependent on the government and the taxes paid by others. This is not only immoral, but also vexing to taxpayers, who may rebel against a system they perceive as unfair.

The concept of federalism, at least as it is practiced in the United States, suggests that different levels of government are best suited for different types of tasks and duties, particularly in terms of charity and poverty amelioration. Local governments (of cities and counties, or parishes in Louisiana) are closest to the problem, and officials at these levels may have the most contact with the people who are actually poor. Because of this, they have the best insight into how to help their neighbors. According to this line of thought, local government should have the final say in how programs are designed and operated. This can lead to huge disparities in treatment, however, and the history of government programs administered at the local level is filled with example after example of discriminatory application of rules and the creation of laws to disallow some groups of people from receiving any benefits.

States actually have a large role in the United States because they are the level of government that is given responsibility for the relief of the poor in the Constitution as one of the rights and duties that was not given to the national government, and so were reserved for the states. While the federal role has expanded greatly in the past 80 years, it has not been a policy option to supersede the states' role entirely. States may or may not choose to delegate the job to local government bodies, but because local government is created by state government, it is ultimately up to the states to determine the scope and limits of local government involvement in these areas. One of the key problems with assigning poverty-reduction efforts to the states, however, is that they quickly begin to diverge in approach. Some states are more generous and some are (much) less generous. This can be a problem from an equity point of view: one's level of relief depends entirely on where one lives, exactly as can occur at the city or county level.

The federal government has a role in poverty relief because it can assure more equitable distribution of funds and opportunities across the entire country, thus eliminating the disparities that otherwise occur. The federal government is also the only level of government that can spend more funds than it receives in any particular accounting period. States and localities are required to have balanced budgets, so when tax revenues fall (due to lack of economic activity or cuts in taxes), expenditures, including for anti-poverty programs, will also be reduced. Thus, when need is usually greatest, during economic recessions, tax collections at the state and local levels are weakest. Only the federal government can keep programs funded regardless of the level of tax receipts. This information argues for more federal government involvement in policies aimed to reduce need.

While all the levels of government have potential reasons to be chosen, the pattern of choice typically is cyclical. At times, legislators pass laws that involve the national government more heavily, and at other times, it is the states or localities that are brought closer to the center of action. The historical perspective brings this type of information to the fore, and situates current policy decisions in the rivers of debate that have flowed for some time. In unsophisticated hands, this model can read as deterministic: because certain factors existed (the desire for change, the ethos of the times, and so on), the policy that emerged is said to be the only result that could be imagined. In this view, a new policy emerges because it was an idea whose time had come and nothing could stand in its way.

The second decision-making model of policy creation is named the "politics and power approach." The key emphasis of this approach is that bargaining takes place among the interested players who each have unequal power and positions. What emerges as the final policy does so as these players use their skills and passion to advocate and receive specific provisions that are then codified into the final legislation, regulation, or statement. This model stresses the dynamic nature of policy-making, no matter the historical context. Nothing is certain, and everything is in play. What matters are the people who are involved. Any other set of people would have caused different results to emerge. Take away any of the key actors in welfare reform, at any level, and President Clinton might have vetoed the third bill sent to him by Congress, reviving Robert Dole's flagging campaign and an unenthusiastic Republican voting base, setting up the loss of the presidency, and changing history as we know it. The power and politics model recognizes the fragile nature of any policy enactment and celebrates the efforts required to achieve it.

The third decision-making model of policy creation is the most easily recognized and is the "rational actor" model. It is a goal-setting, goal-maximizing, economic approach to policy-making, where the key players choose their desired ends and then opt for the most efficient means for achieving them. Bargaining may be required because of the differences in desired ends, but reason is a powerful persuasion tool and can overcome conflicts in values. Policy actors work to fashion win-win scenarios, where compromise and re-framing of options allow more than one player to declare victory.

After reading about these models and their application to the creation of welfare reform legislation in 1996, it is tempting to ask "Which model is best?" The answer is that the selection of the "best" model depends entirely on the purpose of using a model at all. Each model has strengths and weaknesses and is not appropriate for every circumstance. The historical model brings into current debates important information about what has been tried before, why it worked or did not work, and what might be done differently this time to achieve a different effect. It is helpful in the search for alternatives to current policy, particularly when combined with comparative policy analysis. The politics and power model is strong at showing how individuals make a difference, but is weaker in terms of describing where the policy options under consideration come from. It also runs the danger of showing policy-making as devoid of meaning beyond the short-term win. It can be a bit like watching a car chase scene in a movie, not knowing if the police are going to catch the "bad guy" this time, focusing on the police car that might be able to stop the escaping runaway's car, only to fall back, and then struggle to regain the advantage. At some point, the chase is over, and the police have caught their suspect, or not. It is exciting, but misses the point that, in real life, chases are not done just for the sake of having a chase. The bigger picture, that the police want to capture a dangerous criminal, can be lost entirely in a film (in some films, of course, the point of a car chase really is just to add an action sequence). In the case of the politics and power model's description of policy creation, there is frequently a reason for the use of politics and power that is related to a substantive policy disagreement. Unhappily, this is not always true. Sometimes, the exercise of power is simply justified by its holders as being used to ensure that other actors are aware of the power that can be wielded. In such cases, it is vital to have a model such as power and politics that can be used to make sense of the action.

Finally, the rational actor model is best used when it is obvious that the actors have clear policy-related goals and are striving to achieve them. If this is not the case, then it is more difficult, if not impossible, to employ the assumptions of the model. But almost every suggested policy will be backed by at least the appearance of rationality. Even if the logic is found to be lacking by others, there are few decision-makers who cannot develop a logical-sounding rationale for their opinions, policy stances, and votes. A more charitable view of policy-makers is that, even when not all the important assumptions of the rational actor model hold (such as examining all possible alternatives, being able to know with certainty what the results of each alternative would be, and so on), the tenets of bounded rationality do hold: decision-makers, using the information they have about alternatives and outcomes, choose the policy option that best achieves their desired goals. A thorough analysis of any case may show where their knowledge of options or resulting outcomes was flawed, and how that led to errors in achievement of their goals. Still, for the most part, as simple as the approach is, it is useful in showing why certain decisions were made because it takes into account the purposes of the key actors, something neither the historical nor the politics and power models do as strongly.

PROGRAM EVALUATION

One of the important elements of the rational actor model is that it provides a starting place for the evaluation of policies and programs. Goals are presented; they can be operationalized and measured; and the results can be compared to the desired ends. If the goals are met or exceeded, then the policy or program is successful. If the goals are not met, then the policy or program is unsuccessful. The three chapters in Part II each describe different ways to determine systematically and rigorously whether policy goals have been met. Chapter 5 describes qualitative methods; Chapter 6 covers quantitative methods; and Chapter 7 presents mixed methods (combinations of qualitative and quantitative methods) as viable means of collecting information regarding how well policies and programs are being implemented, and the degree to which goals of a policy are being achieved. Within each chapter, a set of criteria was provided to help assess whether any evaluation choosing to use that methodological approach was done well or poorly.

To further underscore the ways program and policy evaluation techniques are used and judged, two examples of evaluation reports related to welfare reform were presented and analyzed in each chapter in Part II. These examples show the variation in scope, cost, and ambitions of what are all program evaluations of some aspect of welfare reform efforts. Despite the strengths of each evaluation, the result of analyzing these examples may be to emphasize the assertion that "All evaluations are imperfect" (Hoefer, 1994, p. 234).

LOOSE ENDS

One element that we have not covered so far in this book is the political nature of program evaluation (Rossi, Lipsey, & Freeman, 2004; Royce, Thyer, & Padgett, 2010) and how the end of the policy process (evaluation) ties back to the beginning of the policy process (creation). According to Weiss (1973) there are three areas where political considerations impact evaluation in important ways:

1. Policies and programs are the result of political decisions;
2. Evaluation reports are part of the information stream used by decision-makers; and
3. Evaluation as a field makes choices about what is important and unimportant, which methods are appropriate and inappropriate, and so on.

All three of these points continue to be valid and are easily seen in the evaluation reports used in the previous chapters. Welfare reform came about as the result of political decisions. The decision-makers who chose the TANF approach used (or, perhaps, misused) information about the AFDC program and how long recipients were on welfare as part of their campaign to end the AFDC program, and evaluators who have approached welfare reform projects have certainly made choices about what to study and in what detail. But let us look closer at Weiss's second point, that evaluation is part of the information stream of policy-making. Rossi et al. (2004) expand on her statement about the impact of politics and evaluation on each other. Evaluation is only one aspect of the policy-making process but potentially an important one. In a democratic form of government, they argue, it is not right for a small group of people to take it upon themselves ultimately to determine the value to the system as a whole of any one program or policy. But because evaluation is a potentially important element of the decision-making process, evaluators must strive to do the best research they can within the limits of budget, time, and ability. Evaluators must strive to make their efforts and reports usable to the multiple stakeholders who may use them.

The nature of social policy-making can, however, burden even the best and most politically savvy of evaluators. Social policies change, even while the evaluation is proceeding (recall the changes in Indiana's AFDC program while the evaluation was going on). In something of an ironic twist, sometimes the policy changes *because* of the evaluation's preliminary findings. Also, to be useful, evaluation results need to be delivered when the data can actually inform a policy decision (Rossi et al., 2004). If the debate is over and the decision-makers' votes are already cast, new evaluation results are of no immediate use.

Another way that evaluations intersect with politics relates to defining success. With welfare reform, one of the most important stated goals was to reduce dependency. This has been used as an overarching element of evaluations ever since the program began. Consistently, evaluations have indicated that the answer is that fewer people are on welfare now than before. Because of this, the policy has been declared "successful." But this conclusion causes a lot of controversy. Some people attack the science behind the evaluations and some directly attack the definition of "success" used. Leaving aside the science of the evaluations attacked (which of course can range from excellent to slipshod), it is more interesting to focus here on the definition of success.

Critics of welfare reform argued that the true purpose of the legislative effort was to make the world safer for big capitalism (Reisch, 2006) or to better control women's bodies and reproductive lives (Abramovitz, 2006). While these were not the stated aims provided within the legislation, it is possible that these were underlying goals, conscious or not. Yet evaluators have not addressed these as being achieved or not, which may be considered as part of Weiss's third intersection of evaluation and policy. A larger issue is to determine who might authoritatively say what the "true" goal of a policy is, in general, and of welfare reform, in particular. The process by which "true goals" are determined is a political process in and of itself, and may lead to critical changes in the policy if a new goal or definition of success is adopted.

This is the point where the policy-creation impetus begins anew, using the information, insights, and interpretations of evaluations to revisit old issues, revise current thinking, and reimagine future possibilities. With the information in this book, readers can become a part of policy-making and evaluation. Understanding how to analyze the creation of any policy prepares participants to intervene successfully in the process. Knowing the ways to evaluate a policy provides readers with the tools to do so and to come to the policy-creation process armed with data and interpretations to support a particular cause. By starting at either of these seemingly loose ends, advocates and evaluators can end up at the other end, following a Mobius strip around in an unending journey to create and evaluate policy in order to improve the lives of human-services clients everywhere.

Glossary

Action research: See "participatory action research."

Aid to Dependent Children (ADC) program: A program created as Title IV of the Social Security Act of 1935 primarily to provide assistance to children who were living in a family without a father present.

Aid to Families with Dependent Children (AFDC) program: A program, begun in 1962, that altered some of the provisions of the ADC program. It provided assistance to parents, even unemployed parents, and states could receive federal reimbursement for some of these costs.

Altruism: A feeling or emotion that puts the needs of others ahead of one's own needs.

Analysis: A systematic and rigorous approach to understanding a phenomenon.

Bounded rationality: An understanding of decision making that states that, due to inherent limitations, people make decisions based on less than perfect information and are prone to adopt the first acceptable alternative ("satisficing"). Thus the tenets of the rational actor model are unrealistic. Nonetheless, this model posits that people still act to achieve their goals as efficiently as possible, given the limits they have on time and other resources.

Checks and balances: The intermixing and balancing of power among government branches such that one branch can prevent other branches from becoming too powerful. (See also "separation of powers.")

Closed-ended question: A question to which respondents choose a response from a list provided to them.

Collective-action problem: A problem facing organizers of group action wherein rational actors will not join because the benefits of joining do not seem to outweigh the costs.

Confirmability: A qualitative methods approach similar to what quantitative researchers call "validity." Confirmability is, in essence, being able to get agreement that events actually occurred.

Constructivism: An approach to knowledge that indicates that reality is not independent of our experience of existence. All persons construct their own reality, based on their own interpretations of what occurs.

Content analysis: This is a type of qualitative data reduction that creates core meanings from a substantial amount of qualitative material.

Convenience sampling: A method of gathering research or evaluation respondents that is based on ease of contact.

Critical approach: An approach to historical policy analysis that emphasizes ever-changing social relations and dependencies. Feminist and Marxist approaches to explaining policy creation use this approach.

Dependency: In the social policy arena, the problem of aid recipients' relying on assistance from others (such as government) for their sustenance rather than relying on their own efforts, such as in the job market.

Deserving poor: A term used to describe people who are poor but who are considered to not be responsible for their own poverty. The type of people who fall into this category can change over time, but usually includes children, the elderly, and people with mental or physical disabilities.

Distributive policy: A type of policy that moves resources from a broad segment of society to a loosely tied set of individuals who receive the benefits. Costs are borne by many, while the rewards are garnered by a select few.

Domestic policy: Government policy aimed primarily at affecting conditions within the country.

Double-barreled question: A closed-ended question item that combines two questions that may have different answers, thus making it impossible to answer accurately.

Elitism: A theory relating to the distribution of power that posits that there is primarily one center of power that is made up of the economic elite in the country, and that government is a biased arbiter in disputes between the power elite and other elements of society, such as the working class. Some elitist theorists believe that multiple elites exist that strive for power.

Experimental design: A type of research design characterized by random assignment of subjects to one of at least two different conditions and thus the use of a control group.

External generalizability: The ability to say that the results of an evaluation or research project from one group or at one time will be similar to another group or at another time. In qualitative research methods, this idea is also known as "extrapolation" or "transferability."

Extrapolation: A qualitative approach to generalizing results from a research project or evaluation to another population, time, or place (see also "transferability"). In quantitative research methods, this idea is called "external generalizability."

Federalism: A system of government that assigns different duties or responsibilities to different levels of government, such as, in the United States, the national government, states, and localities.

Focus group: A face-to-face interview of a small group of people to gather information on a particular topic of interest to the group members and the researcher. Focus groups have the potential to elicit opinions, ideas, beliefs, and impressions that are then commented on by other members of the group. Focus groups are typically made up of people who are rather similar to each other so as to encourage a sense of camaraderie and alikeness.

Foreign policy: Government policy aimed primarily at affecting conditions outside of the national borders.

Grounded theory: A qualitative data-collection approach during which codes or concepts are identified (open coding) then organized into categories or themes (axial coding). During axial coding, constant comparison is used across sources of data (e.g., transcripts of interviews and focus groups, content analysis of policies, observations of policy implementation) to organize codes into the categories and themes.

Hermeneutic approach: A type of historical approach to understanding policy that examines in detail the leaders of countries and organizations to determine what they did and what they believed.

Historical model: An approach to understanding policy that uses credible documents to tell a story about a policy's creation. The historical approach uses remains and testimonies to build a case for any particular interpretation of the way a policy was created.

Institutional power: The amount of power that comes with a person's position in an organization or hierarchy (compare to "personal" power).

Interpretive approach: See "hermeneutic approach."

Interviewing: Interviewing, as a data collection technique, is defined as "a conversation with a purpose" (Berg, 2009, p. 101), with the purpose being to gather information from the interviewee regarding program processes and impacts.

Mixed methods: A research approach that combines both qualitative and quantitative methods.

Naturalistic inquiry: An approach to research and data collection that observes situations as they come about and not through experimental manipulation.

Researchers using this approach remain open to what occurs rather than trying to put situations into a predetermined pattern.

Nomological approach: An approach to historical analysis that looks for generalities in history, seeking to uncover "laws" to explain what has occurred. Using the quantitative techniques of economics and behavioralist social science, people using this approach to history frequently model relationships between dependent and independent variables.

Non-experimental design: A research design that does not use random assignment or a comparison group.

Non-probability sampling: Methods of selecting potential research informants that do not produce a known chance of being included. Types of non-probability sampling include convenience, snowball, quota, and purposive sampling.

Objectivity: In research and evaluation, refers to the ability of the researcher to observe what happens without becoming emotionally involved in what occurs.

Open-ended question: A question to which respondents provide their answer based on what they want to say or write.

Participatory action research (PAR): A type of research or research approach wherein researchers and participants both bring their own skills to the research process to look at a particular problem.

Personal power: The amount of power an individual has due to his or her personal abilities, strengths, weaknesses, interests, and commitments.

Personal Responsibility and Work Opportunity Reconciliation Act of 1996 (PRWORA): Commonly known as the "Welfare Reform Act," this legislation abolished the AFDC program and replaced it with the Temporary Assistance to Needy Families (TANF) program.

Pluralism: A theory relating to the distribution of power that posits that there are multiple centers of power in the country and that government is a fairly neutral arbiter of the relative power of groups active in a particular policy question.

Policy creation: A group process to develop laws, regulations, and statements for authoritative organizations to improve well-being, often using some type of analysis as a means of evidence and persuasion, and usually based on previous policies.

Policy evaluation: The rigorous and systematic collection of information to assess and improve at least one component of a social policy or program (considered in this book as being the same as program evaluation and retrospective or evaluative policy analysis).

Politics and power model: An approach to understanding policy creation that focuses on a "thick description" of the actors' strengths and strategies, the twists and turns of bargaining between them, and the outcomes that emerge from this process.

Pork barrel policy: See "distributive policy."

Positivism: An approach to knowledge that indicates that there is an external reality that can be measured and understood outside of the observer.

Power: The ability to accomplish things (power "to"), or the ability to have other people do what one desires (power "over"), or the ability to keep something from happening or being considered (the "second face" of power).

Principle of less eligibility: The idea that work should always provide greater benefit to an individual than welfare benefits.

Probability sampling: A type of sampling where the probability of being in the sample is known ahead of time. It is possible to generalize to the population from which the sample is drawn when the sample is chosen in this way.

Program: An organized, planned, and usually ongoing effort designed to ameliorate a social problem or improve social conditions.

Program evaluation: The rigorous and systematic collection of information to assess and improve at least one component of a social policy or program (considered in this book as being the same as program evaluation and retrospective or evaluative policy analysis). Program evaluation is also the application of research techniques that is almost always expected to provide a judgment about the degree of implementation of the program that is being studied and/or the extent to which the program achieves the goals assigned to it (compare to "social policy research").

Purposive sampling: A method of gathering respondents based on the researcher's understanding of the situation and knowledge of potential respondents.

Qualitative methods: Research methods that are based on interpretive understandings of the world and accept that reality changes based on the meaning that people bring to it.

Quantitative methods: Research methods that assume that things exist independently of the observer, can be measured (more or less) precisely, and the relationships between variables can be specified with some degree of accuracy or probability.

Quasi-experimental design: A research design that does not use random assignment to a control group but does have a comparison group to improve internal validity.

Quota sampling: A method of gathering respondents based on predetermining a number of respondents possessing certain characteristics, such as gender, age, or level of education.

Redistributive policy: A type of policy where resources are taken from one clearly identified large group of people to distribute to another clearly identified large group of people. The groups are generally large enough to be considered social classes.

Regulatory policy: A type of policy where there is a clear choice between an individual (or class of individuals) who wins and an individual (or class of individuals) who loses, based on general rules or principles.

Reliability: The extent to which multiple measures of a concept by an instrument show similar results.

Remains: A type of source, or evidence, used in the historical approach that is the result of processes such as building, hunting, and cooking.

Representativeness: When describing a source of information, "representativeness" is the degree to which that source is congruent with the full range of sources that exist or once existed.

Sampling: The selection of potential respondents for use in a research project or evaluation. Sampling can use either probability or non-probability techniques.

Secondary data analysis: Using data that were collected for one reason for another research purpose.

Separation of powers: The principle that government power should be divided between different branches. In the United States, three branches share power: the legislative (Congress), the executive (the Presidency), and the judicial (the Courts). When the powers are separated and also intermingled, it is possible that one branch can prevent the others from becoming too powerful (see also "checks and balances").

Snowball sampling: A type of non-probability sampling where the researcher gathers names of potential respondents from current respondents.

Social policy: The laws, regulations, and statements of authoritative organizations to promote well-being.

Social policy creation: A group process to develop laws, regulations, and statements for authoritative organizations to improve well-being, often using some type of analysis as a means of evidence and persuasion, and usually based on previous policies.

Social policy research: The application of (qualitative and/or quantitative) research techniques to the topic of social policy.

Social welfare policy: Policies that affect the distribution of resources in a society.

Stages model of policy-making: An heuristic approach to understanding the steps of the policy process. The names of the stages depend on the author cited but frequently move from the first stage, where an issue emerges, to a final stage, where evaluation of the policy occurs. Authors then see the evaluation leading back into a possible new round of policy-making, beginning at the issue-emergence stage again.

Standardized measure: An instrument that has been previously tested in order to have known levels of reliability and validity with certain populations.

Survey research: A research technique that involves asking respondents questions, either in written form or verbally.

Temporary Assistance to Needy Families (TANF) program: The program created in the 1996 Personal Responsibility and Work Opportunity Reconciliation Act that replaced the AFDC program to provide assistance to low-income families.

Testimonies of witnesses: Reports (which can be written or oral) that describe events.

Theoretical sampling: An approach in qualitative research to improve the representativeness of the research being conducted by choosing particular respondents on the basis of concepts that are emerging. The respondents are chosen so as to be able to provide information regarding the new concepts, rather than being chosen based on probability sampling techniques, such as random selection.

Transferability: In qualitative research, the fit between results from one group of people to another group of people (similar to generalizability in quantitative research). (See also "extrapolation.")

Transparency: The idea of the researcher's discussing his or her own biases. This is important because the researcher is the data-collection instrument and interpreter. Only by understanding the patterns of belief and thoughts that the qualitative researcher brings to the project can they be taken into account by the consumer of the research.

Triangulation: The use of more than one method to collect data. Triangulation can occur when more than one instrument is used, more than one theoretical orientation is used, or more than one researcher is used.

Undeserving poor: A term used to describe people who are poor but who are considered to be responsible for their own poverty, perhaps because they are not willing to work at the jobs that are available to them and for which they are qualified.

Unworthy poor: See "undeserving poor."

Validity: A property of a measure indicating that it collects the information that it is designed to collect. A valid measure is one that is "true" because it measures what it sets out to measure.

Welfare Reform Law: See "Personal Responsibility and Work Opportunity Reconciliation Act."

Worthy poor: See "deserving poor."

References

Abramovitz, M. (2006). Neither accidental, nor simply mean-spirited: The context for welfare reform. In K. Kilty and E. Segal (Eds.), *The promise of welfare reform: Political rhetoric and the reality of poverty in the twenty-first century* (pp. 23–37). New York: Haworth Press.

Alcock, P. (2008). The subject of social policy. In P. Alcock, M. May, and K. Rowlingson, *The student's companion to social policy*, (3rd ed.), (pp. 3–10). Malden, MA: Blackwell Publishing.

Allen, A. (2005). Feminist perspectives on power. *Stanford Encyclopedia of Philosophy*, retrieved from http://plato.stanford.edu/entries/feminist-power/.

Allison, G. (1971). *Essence of decision: Explaining the Cuban missile crisis* (1st ed.). Boston: Little, Brown & Company.

Allison, G., and Zelikow, P. (1999). *Essence of decision: Explaining the Cuban missile crisis* (2nd ed.). New York: Longman.

Ambrosino, R., Heffernan, J., Shuttlesworth, G., and Ambrosino, R. (2008). *Social work and social welfare: An introduction* (6th ed.). Boston: Allyn & Bacon.

Anderson, M. (1978). *Welfare: The political economy of welfare reform in the United States.* Stanford, CA: Hoover Institution Press.

Bachrach, P., and Baratz, M. (1962). Two faces of power. *The American Political Science Review, 57*, 632–642.

Banks, S. (1992). *Exploratory modeling and the use of simulation for policy analysis.* Santa Monica, CA: Rand.

Bardach, E. (2005). *A practical guide for policy analysis* (2nd ed.). Washington, DC: CQ Press.

Barusch, A. (2006). *Foundations of social policy: Social justice in human perspective* (2nd ed.). Pacific Grove, CA: Brooks/Cole.

Baum, E. (1991). When the witch doctors agree: The Family Support Act and social science research. *Journal of Policy Analysis and Management 10* (Fall), 603–615.

Beecroft, E., Cahill, K., and Goodson, B. (2002). *The impacts of welfare reform on children: The Indiana welfare reform evaluation.* Bethesda, MD: Abt Associates. Retrieved from http://www.abtassociates.com/reports/ES-Indy_Child_Final_Report.pdf.

Beecroft, E., Lee, W., and Long, D. (2003). *The Indiana welfare reform evaluation: Five-year impacts, implementation, costs, and benefits.* Bethesda, MD: Abt Associates. Retrieved from http://www.abtassociates.com/reports/indiana_final_report.pdf.

Berg, B. (2009). *Qualitative research methods for the social sciences* (7th ed.). Boston: Allyn & Bacon.

Bernheimer, L., Weisner, T., and Lowe, E. (2003). Impacts of children with troubles on working poor families: Mixed-method and experimental evidence. *Mental Retardation, 41*(6): 403–419.

Best, J. (2001). *Damned lies and statistics.* Berkeley: University of California Press.

Birkland, T. (2005). *An introduction to the policy process: Theories, concepts, and models of public policy making* (2nd ed.). Armonk, NY: M.E. Sharpe.

Blau, J. (2006). Welfare reform in historical perspective. In K. Kilty and E. Segal (Eds.), *The promise of welfare reform: Political rhetoric and the reality of poverty in the twenty-first century* (pp. 49–56). New York: Haworth Press.

Blau, J. (with Abramowitz, M.) (2004). *The dynamics of social welfare policy.* New York: Oxford University Press.

Blau, J. (with Abramovitz, M.) (2010). *The dynamics of social welfare policy* (3rd ed.). New York: Oxford University Press.

Bloom, D., Scrivener, S., Michalopoulos, C., Morris, P., Hendra, R., Adams-Ciardullo, D., and Walter, J. (with Vargas, W.) (2002). *Jobs first: Final report on Connecticut's welfare reform initiative.* New York: Manpower Demonstration Research Corporation.

Blumenthal, S. (2003). *The Clinton wars.* New York: Farrar, Straus & Giroux.

Bos, J., Huston, A., Granger, R., Duncan, G., Brock, T., and McLoyd, V. (1999). *New hope for people with low incomes.* New York: Manpower Demonstration Research Corporation.

Boyer, G. (1990). *An economic history of the English Poor Law.* New York: Cambridge University Press.

Bureau of Labor Statistics, United States Department of Labor (2003). *American labor in the twentieth century.* Retrieved from www.bls.gov/opub/cwc/cm20030124ar02p1.htm.

Burham, P., Lutz, K., Grant, W., and Layton-Henry, Z. (2008). *Research methods in politics* (2nd ed.). New York: Palgrave Macmillan.

Burke, V., and Burke, V. (1974). *Nixon's good deed: Welfare reform.* New York: Columbia University Press.

Buros Institute of Mental Measurement (2007). *The mental measurements yearbook.* New York: Ovid Technologies.

Butler, S., Corbett, J., Bond, C., and Hastedt, C. (2008). Long-term TANF participants and barriers to employment: A qualitative study in Maine. *Journal of Sociology and Social Welfare, 35*(3): 49–69.

Campbell, D., and Stanley, J. (1963). *Experimental and quasi-experimental designs for research.* Chicago: Rand McNally College.

Campbell, R., Pound, P., Pope, C., Britten, N., Pill, R., Morgan, M., and Donovan, J. (2003). Evaluating meta-ethnography: A synthesis of qualitative research on lay experiences of diabetes and diabetes care. *Social Science and Medicine, 56,* 671–684.

CBS News (January 16, 2009). *The Bush legacy.* Bush's final approval rating: 22 percent. Retrieved from http://www.cbsnews.com/stories/2009/01/16/opinion/polls/main4728399.shtml.

Chambers, D., and Wedel, K. (2008). *Social policy and social programs: A method for the practical public policy analyst* (5th ed.). Boston: Allyn & Bacon.

Clinton, W. (1996). *Statement by President Clinton on welfare reform legislation.* White House Briefing Room, 2:26 P.M. EDT, Wednesday, July 31, 1996. Federal News Service. Retrieved from http://www.fednews.com/transcripta.htm?id=19960731z0347&query=Clinton|welfare|reform.

Dahl, R. (1957). The concept of power. *Behavioral Science, 2,* 201–215.

Dahl, R. (1961). *Who governs? Democracy and power in an American city.* New Haven, CT: Yale University Press.

Danziger, S. (1999). *Welfare reform policy.* What role for social science? Paper prepared for conference, "The Social Sciences and Policy Making," Institute for Social Research, University of Michigan, March 13–14, 1998 (revised December 1999).

Data and Information Services Center (2003). An introduction to using data at DISC. Retrieved from http://www.disc.wisc.edu/types/secondary.htm.

Day, P. (2008). *A new history of social welfare* (6th ed.). Boston: Allyn & Bacon.

Dear, R. (1995). Social welfare policy. In R. Edwards (Ed.), *Encyclopedia of social work* (19th ed.) (pp. 2226–2237). Washington, DC: NASW Press.

Denzin, N. (2002). The interpretive process. In A. M. Huberman and M. Miles (Eds.), *The qualitative researcher's companion* (pp. 349–366). Thousand Oaks, CA: Sage Publications.

Devine, F. (2002). Qualitative methods. In D. Marsh and Gerry Stoker (Eds), *Theory and methods in political science* (2nd ed.). (pp. 197–215). New York: Palgrave.

Derthick, M. (1975). *Uncontrollable spending for social services grants*. Washington, DC: Brookings Institute.

Dictionary.com (2010). S.v. Create. Retrieved from http://dictionary.reference.com/browse/create.

DiNitto, D. (with Cummins, L.) (2007). *Social welfare: Politics and public policy* (6th ed.). Boston: Allyn & Bacon.

Dolbeare, K. and Lidman, R. (1985). Ideology and policy research: The case of Murray's Losing Ground. *Review of Policy Resarch, 4*(4), 587–594.

Dudley, J. (2010). *Research methods for social work* (2nd ed.). Boston: Allyn & Bacon.

Feinstein, C., and Thomas, M. (2002). *Making history count: A primer in quantitative methods for historians*. New York: Cambridge University Press.

Fetterman, D., and Wandersman, A. (2004). *Empowerment evaluation principles in practice*. New York: Guildford Press.

Finfgeld, D. (2003). Metasynthesis: The state of the art—so far. *Qualitative Health Research, 13*(7): 893–904.

Finfgeld-Connett, D. (2010). Generalizability and transferability of metasynthesis research findings. *Journal of Advanced Nursing, 66*(2): 246–254.

Fischer, J., and Corcoran, K. (2007). *Measures for clinical practice and research* (4th ed.). New York: Oxford University Press.

Frogner, B., Moffitt, R., and Ribar, D. (2009). How families are doing nine years after welfare reform: 2005 evidence from the Three-City Study. In J. Ziliak (Ed.), *Welfare reform and its long term consequences for America's poor* (pp. 140–171). New York: Cambridge University Press.

From, A. (July 17, 1995). How Democrats can seize the initiative on welfare reform. Available at DLC Forum, http://www.dlc.org/ndol_ci.cfm?kaid=127&subid=176&contentid=2083.

Gallop Poll (January 14, 2009). *Bush presidency closes with 34% approval, 64% disapproval*. http://www.gallup.com/poll/113770/Bush-Presidency-Closes-34-Approval-61-Disapproval.aspx.

Gilbert, N., and Terrell, P. (2009). *Dimensions of social welfare policy* (7th ed.). Boston: Allyn & Bacon.

Gillon, S. (2008). *The pact: Bill Clinton, Newt Gingrich, and the rivalry that defined a generation*. New York: Oxford University Press.

Gingrich, N. (2005). *Winning the future: A twenty-first century contract with America*. Washington: Regnery Publishing.

Gordon, M. (2009). *Social security policies in industrial countries: A comparative analysis*. Cambridge; New York: Cambridge University Press.

Gupta, D. (2001). *Analyzing public policy: Concepts, tools and techniques*. Washington, DC: CQ Books.

Hamilton, N. (2007). *Bill Clinton: Mastering the presidency.* New York: Public Affairs Books.

Harrington, M. (1962; republished in 1997). *The other America.* New York: Touchstone Press.

Harris, J. (2005). *The survivor: Bill Clinton in the White House.* New York: Random House.

Haskins, R. (1991). Congress writes a law: Research and welfare reform. *Journal of Policy Analysis and Management, 10* (Fall): 616–632.

Haskins, R. (2006). *Work over welfare: The inside story of the 1996 welfare reform law.* Washington, DC: Brookings Institution Press.

Haskins, R. (2006). Welfare reform 10 years later. Brookings Institute. Retrieved from http://www.brookings.edu/interviews/2006/0824welfare_haskins.aspx.

Hill, M. (2006). *Social policy in the modern world: A comparative text.* Malden, MA; Oxford, UK: Wiley/Blackwell.

Hoefer, R. (1994). A good story, well told: Rules for evaluating human services programs. *Social Work, 39*(2): 233–236.

Howell, M., and Prevenier, W. (2001). *From reliable sources: An introduction to historical methods.* Ithaca, NY: Cornell University Press.

Hudson, J., and Lowe, S. (2009). *Understanding the policy process: Analyzing welfare policy and practice* (2nd ed.). Bristol, UK: The Policy Press.

Institute for Research on Poverty (2005). *Current qualitative research. Qualitative approaches to the study of poverty and welfare reform: Current challenges.* Retrieved from http://www.irp.wisc.edu/newsevents/conferences/qualitative.htm#current.

Jansson, B. (2008). *The reluctant welfare state: Engaging history to advance social work practice in contemporary society* (6th ed.). Pacific Grove, CA: Brooks Cole.

Jones, B., Boushey, G., and Workman, S. (2006). Behavioral rationality and the policy processes: Toward a new model of organizational information processing (pp. 49–74). In B. Guy Peters and J. Pierre, *Handbook of public policy.* Thousand Oaks, CA: Sage.

Joseph, A., Jr. (2006). Welfare reform: Forward to the past. In K. Kilty and E. Segal, E. (Eds.), *The promise of welfare reform: Political rhetoric and the reality of poverty in the twenty-first century* (pp. 1–4). New York: Haworth Press.

Karger, H., and Stoesz, D. (2010). *American social welfare policy: A pluralist approach* (6th ed.). Boston: Allyn & Bacon.

Kilty, K., and Segal, E. (2006). Introduction. In K. Kilty and E. Segal (Eds.), *The promise of welfare reform: Political rhetoric and the reality of poverty in the twenty-first century* (pp. 1–4). New York: Haworth Press.

Kindon, S., Pain, R., and Kesby, M. (2007). Introduction: Connecting people, participation and place. In S. Kindon, R. Pain, and M. Kesby (Eds.), *Participatory action research approaches and methods: Connecting people, participation and place* (pp. 1–5). New York: Routledge.

Knab, J., Garfinkel, I., McLanahan, S., Moiduddin, E., and Osborne, C. (2009). The effects of welfare and child support policies on the incidence of marriage following a nonmarital birth. In J. Ziliak, (Ed.), *Welfare reform and its long term consequences for America's poor* (pp. 290–307). New York: Cambridge University Press.

Lee, W., Beecroft, E., Khadurri, J., and Patterson, R. (2003). *Impacts of Welfare Reform on Recipients of Housing Assistance: Evidence from Indiana and Delaware.* Bethesda MD: Abt Associates Inc.

Lindblom, C. (1959). The science of muddling through. *Public Administration Review, 19,* 78–88.

Lincoln, Y., and Guba, E. (1985). Establishing trustworthiness. In Y. Lincoln and E. Guba, *Naturalistic Inquiry* (pp. 289–331). Thousand Oaks, CA: Sage.

Lipsky, M. (1980). *Street-level bureaucracy: Dilemmas of the individual in public services.* New York: Russell Sage Foundation.

London, A., Schwartz, S., and Scott, E. (2006). Combining quantitative and qualitative data in welfare policy evaluation in the United States. *World Development, 35*(2): 342–353.

Lott, T. (2005). *Herding cats: A life in politics.* New York: Harper Collins Publishers.

Lowi, T. (1964). American business, public policy, case-studies, and political theory. *World Politics. 16*(4): 677–715.

Luprest, P. (1996). *Supplemental Security Income for children with disabilities.* Washington, DC: Urban Institute.

Mandell, B. (1995). Why can't we care for our own children? *Feminist Economics, 1*(2): 99–104.

March, J. (1994). *A primer on decision-making.* New York: Free Press.

March, J., and Simon, H. (1958). *Organizations.* New York: Wiley and Sons.

Mathison, S. (2008). What is the difference between evaluation and research—and why do we care? In N. Smith and P. Brandon (Eds.), *Fundamental issues in evaluation* (pp. 183–196). New York: Guildford Press.

McNabb, D. (2004). *Research methods for political science: Quantitative and qualitative methods.* Armonk, NY: M.E. Sharpe.

Mead, L. (1986). *Beyond entitlement: The social obligations of citizenship.* New York: Basic Books.

Mead, L. (1992). *The new politics of poverty: The non-working poor in America.* New York: Basic Books.

Mindel, C., and Hoefer, R. (2006). An evaluation of a family strengthening program for substance abuse offenders. *Journal of Social Service Research,* *32*(4): 23–38.

Murray, C. (1984). *Losing ground: American social policy, 1950–1980.* New York: Basic Books.

Morris, D. and McGann, E. (2004). *Because he could.* New York: HarperCollins Publishers.

Nelson, M. (2006). Lessons from Vermont. In K. Kilty and E. Segal, E. (Eds.), *The promise of welfare reform: Political rhetoric and the reality of poverty in the twenty-first century* (pp. 23–37). New York: Haworth Press.

Neustadt, R. (1990). *Presidential power and the modern presidents: The politics of leadership from Roosevelt to Reagan* (5th ed.). New York: Free Press.

Ney, S. (2009). *Resolving messy policy problems: Handling conflict in environmental, transport, health and aging policy.* Sterling, VA: Earthscan.

Nixon, R. (1969). Welfare reform: A message from the President of the United States. House Document No. 91–146, *Congressional Record,* Vol. 115, no. 136, The House of Representatives, 91st Congress, First Session, H7239–7241.

Office of Human Services Policy (1998). *Aid to Families with Dependent Children: A baseline.* Retrieved from http://aspe.hhs.gov/hsp/afdc/afdchase98.htm.

Office of Human Services Policy (2009). *Aid to Families with Dependent Children and Temporary Assistance to Needy Families Overview.* Retrieved from http://aspe.hhs.gov/hsp/abbrev/afdc-tanf.htm.

Ohlson, C. (1998). Welfare reform: Implications for young children with disabilities, their families, and service providers. *Journal of Early Intervention, 21,* 191–206.

Olson, M. (1965). The logic of collective action: Public goods and the theory of groups. Cambridge, MA: Harvard University Press.

Orr, J. (2000). *Faith-Based Organizations and Welfare Reform: California Religious Community Capacity Study: Qualitative Findings and Conclusions.* Los Angeles: Center for Religion and Civic Culture, University of Southern California.

Paden, C., and Page, B. (2003). Congress invokes public opinion on welfare reform. *American Politics Research, 31*(6), pp. 670–9. DOI: 10.1177/1532673X03255181.

Padgett, D. (2008). *Qualitative methods in social work research* (2nd ed.). Thousand Oaks, CA: Sage Publications.

Patton, C., and Sawicki, D. (1986). *Basic methods of policy analysis and planning.* Englewood Cliffs, NJ: Prentice-Hall.

Patton, C., and Sawicki, D. (1993). *Basic methods of policy analysis and planning* (2nd ed.). New York: Prentice-Hall.

Patton, M. (2002). *Qualitative research and evaluation methods* (3rd ed.). Thousand Oaks, CA: Sage Publications.

Peck, L., and Gershon, S. (2006). Welfare reform and the American dream. In K. Kilty and E. Segal, (Eds.), *The promise of welfare reform: Political rhetoric and the reality of poverty in the twenty-first century* (97–120). New York: Haworth Press.

Popple, P., and Leighninger, L. (2008). *The policy-based profession: An introduction to social welfare policy analysis for social workers* (4th ed.). Boston: Allyn & Bacon.

Rachel Maddow Show (March 31, 2010). Interview with Chris Hayes. Video retrieved from http://videocafe.crooksandliars.com/heather/rachel-maddow-president-obamas-compromise.

Read, M., and Marsh, D. (2002). Combining quantitative and qualitative methods. In D. Marsh and G. Stoker (Eds.), *Theory and methods in political science* (2nd ed.), (pp. 231–248). New York: Palgrave.

Reisch, M. (2006). Welfare reform and the transformation of the U.S. welfare state. In K. Kilty and E. Segal, E. (Eds.), *The promise of welfare reform: Political rhetoric and the reality of poverty in the twenty-first century* (pp. 69–80). New York: Haworth Press.

Reisch, M., and Gorin, S. (2000). The nature of work and the future of the social work profession. *Social Work, 46*(1): 9–19.

Rihoux, B. (2006). *Innovative comparative methods for policy analysis: Beyond the quantitative-qualitative divide.* New York: Springer US.

Rosman, E. A., and Knitzer, J. (2001). Welfare reform: The special case of young children with disabilities and their families. *Infants and Young Children, 13,* 25–35.

Rossi, P., Lipsey, M., Freeman, H. (2004). *Evaluation: A systematic approach* (7th ed.). Thousand Oaks, CA: Sage.

Royce, D., Thyer, B, and Padgett, D. (2010). *Program evaluation: An introduction* (5th ed.). Belmont, CA: Wadsworth.

Rubin, A. and Babbie, E. (2008). *Research methods for social work* (6th ed.). Belmont, CA: Thomson Brooks/Cole.

Sandelowski, M. (1995). Sample size in qualitative research. *Research in Nursing and Health, 18,* 179–183.

Sadler, D. R. (1981). Intuitive data processing as a potential source of bias in naturalistic evaluations. *Educational Evaluation and Policy Analysis, 3*(4): 25–31.

Schiller, B. (2007). *The economics of poverty and discrimination* (10th ed). Upper Saddle River, NJ: Prentice Hall.

Schofield, J. (1990). Increasing the generalizability of qualitative research. In E. Eisner and A. Peshkin (Eds.), *Qualitative inquiry in education* (pp. 201–232). New York: Teachers College Press.

Skocpol, T. (1995). *Protecting soldiers and mothers: The political origins of social policy in the United States.* Cambridge, MA: Harvard University Press.

Simon, H. (1982). *Models of bounded rationality.* Cambridge, MA: MIT Press.

Simon, H. (1985). Human nature in politics: The dialogue of psychology with political science. *American Political Science Review, 79,* 293–304.

Spano, R. (2000). Creating the context for the analysis of social policies: Understanding the historical context. In D. Chambers, *Social policy and social programs: A method for the practical public policy analyst* (3rd ed.), (pp. 31–45). Boston: Allyn & Bacon.

Stewart, D., and Shamdasani, P. (1990). *Focus groups: Theory and practice.* Thousand Oaks, CA: Sage.

Tanner, M.D. (August 21, 2006). The critics were wrong: Welfare reform turns 10. Retrieved from The Cato Institute Web site: http://www.cato.org/pub_display.php?pub_id=6629.

Trattner, W. (1998). *From Poor Law to welfare state: A history of social welfare in America* (6th ed.). New York: Free Press.

United States Census Bureau (September 2010). *Poverty: 2008 and 2009: American Community Survey briefs.* Retrieved from http://www.census.gov/prod/2010pubs/acsbr09–1.pdf.

United States Department of Health and Human Services (September 1996). *The Personal Responsibility and Work Opportunity Reconciliation Act of 1996.* Retrieved from http://aspe.hhs.gov/hsp/abbrev/prwora96.htm.

United States House of Representatives (1994a). *Contract with America.* http://www.house.gov/house/Contract/CONTRACT.html.

United States House of Representatives (1994b). *The Personal Responsibility Act: Highlights.* http://www.house.gov/house/Contract/persrespd.txt.

Veit-Wilson, J. (2000). States of welfare: A conceptual challenge. *Social Policy and Administration, 34*(1): 1–25.

Vobeja, B., and Balz, D. (August 22, 1996). President seeks balm for anger over welfare bill. *The Washington Post,* p. A1.

Walsh, J., and Corcoran, J. (2006). Motivational interviewing. In J. Walsh, *Theories for direct social work practice* (2nd ed.), (pp. 253–272). Belmont, CA: Wadsworth Cengage.

Ward, H. (2003). Rational choice. In D. Marsh and G. Stoker (Eds.), *Theory and methods in political science* (3rd ed.), (pp. 65–89). Basingstoke, UK: Palgrave Macmillan.

Weiss, C. (1973). Where politics and evaluation research meet. *Evaluation Practice, 14*(1): 9–106.

Yanow, D. (2006a). Neither rigorous nor objective? Interrogating criteria for knowledge claims in interpretive science. In D. Yanow and P. Schwartz-Shea

(2006), *Interpretation and method: Empirical research methods and the interpretive turn* (pp. 67–88). Armonk, NY: M.E. Sharpe.

Yanow, D. (2006b). Thinking interpretively: Philosophical presuppositions and the human sciences. In D. Yanow and P. Schwartz-Shea (2006), *Interpretation and method: Empirical research methods and the interpretive turn* (pp. 5–26). Armonk, NY: M.E. Sharpe.

Zukerman, D. (2000). Welfare reform in America: A clash of politics and research. *Journal of Social Issues, 56*(4): 587–599.

Index